janella's
WHOLEFOOD KITCHEN

ALLEN&UNWIN

First published in 2012

Allen & Unwin
Sydney, Melbourne, Auckland, London

83 Alexander Street
Crows Nest NSW 2065
Australia
Phone: (61 2) 8425 0100
Email: info@allenandunwin.com
Web: www.allenandunwin.com

Cataloguing-in-Publication details are available
from the National Library of Australia
www.trove.nla.gov.au

ISBN 978 1 74331 098 4

Internal design by Liz Seymour
Photography by Heath Missen
Food preparation by Luke Southwood and Janella Purcell
Styling by Janella Purcell
Index by Jo Rudd

Colour reproduction by Splitting Image, Clayton, Victoria
Printed in China, produced by Phoenix Offset

10 9 8 7 6 5 4 3 2 1

This book is dedicated to all of you who continually encourage and support me on my wholefood mission. Thank you, from my heart.

LIVE EACH SEASON AS IT PASSES;
BREATHE THE AIR, DRINK THE DRINK,
TASTE THE FRUIT, AND RESIGN YOURSELF
TO THE INFLUENCES OF EACH.

~ HENRY DAVID THOREAU

Contents

Introduction

SLOW FOOD – Seasonal, Local, Organic and Whole.

'Wellness' is something I spend a lot of time contemplating.
And what I have learned is that it's not just about one thing.

Good health requires a holistic and long-term approach. We need clean water, organic food, enough sleep, appropriate exercise, positive relationships and less stress. It might seem like an unachievable to-do list at this moment in your life, but guess what? It's not. The first step to becoming your future optimum self begins in the kitchen. Once you have your diet sorted then you can tackle the rest, one step at a time.

You don't need a quick-fix diet or app to reduce your cholesterol, weight, blood pressure or blood sugar, or to make you happier or to enjoy a better sex life. All you need to do is to take responsibility for your health and realise that you are in charge of it. This begins with what you put in your mouth.

I use organic produce where possible and I strongly encourage you to do the same. But if you can't or don't choose to, eating from my Wholefood Kitchen will still provide benefits for you.

Good health starts in your kitchen. I firmly believe in the medicinal power of food and how it heals not only physically, but mentally and spiritually. A healthy relationship with food and knowing what and how to eat properly is my goal for you. And it really isn't hard or expensive.

I find I'm far less likely to let organic produce go bad sitting in the bottom of the fridge or at the back of the pantry. If you eat good-quality wholefood, you will eat much less, so that means you will buy less and ultimately waste less.

In buying organic and local food you are supporting your local farmers, and reducing your carbon footprint and the amount of toxic chemicals going into your body. Just as importantly – and best of all – you'll be eating in season, which gives you tastier, fresher produce.

The recipes in this book will help improve the condition of your heart; balance your blood sugar; reduce excess fat and help you maintain a healthy weight; they will decrease your chances of getting cancer or help you deal with the condition; reduce arthritis; improve digestive issues; decrease anxiety and depression; assist with behavioural issues in children and adults; improve fertility and reproductive health; increase your energy levels and your quality of sleep; give you glowing skin, shiny hair and healthy teeth and gums; improve your immunity; reduce

free radical build-up and so much more. Big claims, aren't they? But I stand by them. I've had my own naturopathic practice for many years and food as medicine plays a large part of the treatments and support I offer. I see the results in my clients.

Most of my recipes are gluten free, dairy free, vegan and vegetarian, and you'll see a code next to the recipe title so you can easily differentiate. Some recipes use only raw food, and I have noted these also.

DF – DAIRY FREE; GF – GLUTEN FREE; R – RAW; V – VEGETARIAN; VG – VEGAN

Those of you who have followed my journey in *Elixir* and *Eating for the Seasons* will know that my relationship with food was not always an easy one. We are now good friends and I have made it my life's purpose to teach others how to achieve this kind of loving relationship. As George Bernard Shaw said, 'There is no love sincerer than the love of food'.

Welcome to my organic, wholefood kitchen. It's a fun, yummy, empowering and healthy place to be.

In My Kitchen

These are the ingredients I tend to use the most frequently.
Of course there are plenty of others, but these are my favourites.

PANTRY

Oils – olive, rice bran, coconut, sesame, lemon-infused olive oil, macadamia, walnut, avocado

Vinegars – umeboshi, balsamic, white and red wine, apple cider, shaoxing rice wine

Salt – Celtic, Himalayan, Murray River, sea salt

Pepper – white and black

Sweeteners – coconut palm sugar, panela, agave, maple syrup, rice syrup, raw honey

Spices – saffron, paprika (hot, sweet and smoked), cumin, garam masala, turmeric, coriander seeds, dried chilli flakes, sumac, dukkah, cardamom, vanilla beans, allspice

Essences and extracts – rosewater, orange blossom water, natural vanilla extract

Flours – spelt, brown rice, besan, amaranth, quinoa

Grains, noodles and crackers – amaranth, millet, brown rice, buckwheat, spelt, quinoa (although technically a seed)

Nuts – raw and toasted, unsalted, mixed

Dried fruit – goji berries, dates, cranberries, mangoes, figs, raisins

Milk – almond, rice, quinoa, hazelnut, oat, soy (whole beans)

Seeds – pepitas, sunflower, sesame, linseeds, chia

Sauces and seasonings – tamari, fish sauce, mirin

Seaweeds – nori, arame, kombu, wakame, korengo fronds, agar agar

Raw cacao powder

Coconut – milk, flakes, shredded and desiccated

Anchovy fillets

Miso paste – shiro, genmai, hatcho

Nut and seed butters – macadamia, almond, hazelnut, tahini, flaxseed

Canned legumes – chickpeas, navy, cannellini, adzuki, kidney and borlotti beans

Dried lentils – puy or tiny blue-green, whole green/brown, split red and green, mung dal

Flatbread

Dried shiitake mushrooms

FRIDGE

Spices – fresh ginger, turmeric, chillies, lemongrass, kaffir lime leaves

Herbs – coriander, thyme, mint, basil, chives, parsley, rosemary

Eggs – free range and organic

Veggies – sweet potato, beetroot, pumpkin, broccoli, red and green cabbage, spring onions, French and red Asian shallots, fennel, snow peas, green beans, mushrooms, corn, zucchini, radishes, carrots

Dark green leafy veggies – rocket, kale, baby and English spinach, silverbeet, Asian greens

Oils – flaxseed

Sprouts – buckwheat, radish, alfalfa, sunflower

Fruit – blueberries, apples, oranges, mango, pomegranate, papaya, anything organic and seasonal

Tofu – firm, soft, silken, smoked

Dairy – goat's milk and cheese

BENCH

Garlic – Australian organic, pink

Onions – red, white and brown

Lemons and limes

Avocados

FREEZER

Stock – vegetable, seafood

Kaffir lime leaves

FAVOURITE UTENSILS

You don't need loads of pots, pans, gadgets, boards, knives and other things in your kitchen. As with all things, keep it simple, have only what you use, and buy the best you can afford. Avoid anything plastic (unless it states it's safe/chemical-free plastic) as it contains toxic chemicals that can leach into your food. Also avoid Teflon and aluminium in any form, and don't have a microwave in your home. Microwaves give off radioactive waves that are damaging to your health and may be cancer causing.

Zester

Microplane

Fine sieve

Spice grinder

One good, large flat-edged knife

One small knife

Mandoline

Flat, large peeler

Soft, rubber spatula

Stainless-steel mixing bowls

Wooden cutting boards, two or three different-sized ones

Soup ladle

Serving spoons, two or three

Hand-held blender

Food processor

Blender (not essential if you have a hand-held blender)

Stainless-steel pots and pans

Cast-iron pan

Mouli for puréeing and making stock

Glass storage containers with lids for both the pantry and fridge

BREAKFAST

Breakfast should be the biggest and most nutritious meal of the day. As Adelle Davis said, 'Eat breakfast like a king, lunch like a prince, and dinner like a pauper.' Try to never skip breakfast, and preferably take your time eating it. In order to keep you going through to lunchtime, be sure your breakfast contains some form of protein – like eggs, oats, fish, amaranth, quinoa, spelt, miso paste, nuts or nut milk – or legumes like baked beans, hummus or tofu. Protein keeps us feeling fuller longer and helps with brain activity. I also recommend that you include whole grains like spelt, quinoa, flatbread, brown rice, rye or oats in your breakfast. Whole grains keep your blood sugar even for longer, and they also contain loads of fibre for good digestive health.

GORGEOUS GLUTEN-FREE MUESLI

LUMMUR

CORN AND EGG TORTILLA

ALMOND AND BANANA PANCAKES

CONGEE WITH SHIITAKE AND GOMASHIO

CREAMY HERBED MUSHROOMS ON RYE SOURDOUGH

SARDINES ON TOAST

QUINOA PORRIDGE

THE ULTIMATE BREAKFAST SMOOTHIE

NEVER WORK BEFORE BREAKFAST; IF YOU HAVE TO WORK BEFORE BREAKFAST, EAT YOUR BREAKFAST FIRST. ~ JOSH BILLINGS

Gorgeous Gluten-free Muesli
(DF, GF, V, VG)

This will take you just a few minutes to mix up. It is economical, satisfying and so tasty. Experiment with different dried fruits and nuts. Be sure the dried fruit is organic, or at least sulphur free.

SERVES 4–6

1 cup puffed amaranth, millet
   or quinoa
2 cups organic cornflakes
¼ cup sunflower seeds
¼ cup pepitas
½ cup LSA
¼ cup hazelnuts, or any nut, roughly
   chopped
½ cup goji berries or dried cranberries
soy or rice milk, to serve

In a large bowl, mix all the ingredients together.

Serve the muesli with soy or rice milk.

Your muesli will last for up to a month in an airtight container in your pantry or even longer in your fridge.

Lummur (DF)

On the third Thursday in April, Iceland celebrates the first day of summer. Lummur are served on this day. They are similar to pancakes but are heavier, thanks to the oats. This is my version. Serve without the salmon for a vegetarian and vegan alternative. You can also use quark instead of the coconut milk yoghurt but then the dish won't be dairy free.

MAKES 8 PANCAKES

1½ cups cooked oat meal, cooled
½ cup spelt or brown rice flour
1 tsp ground cardamom
1 tsp grated coconut palm sugar
½ tsp sea salt
1 tsp low-allergy baking powder
1 egg
1 cup rice or soy milk
smoked salmon, coconut milk
   yoghurt and slices of cucumber; or
   fruit such as peaches, berries or kiwi
   fruit and honey (or maple syrup);
   to serve
2 tbsp macadamia, coconut or rice
   bran oil

Place the oat meal in a bowl, then sift in the flour, cardamom, sugar, salt and baking powder. Next, stir in the egg and milk.

Heat 1 teaspoon oil in a frying pan over medium heat, pour in about ½ cup of batter and cook until tiny bubbles appear on the surface and the bottom is golden brown, then flip. Cook this side until golden, then transfer to a plate and keep warm. Using a little more oil, repeat with the remaining batter.

Stack the lummur on a plate and serve topped with smoked salmon, cucumber and yoghurt, or with fruit and honey or maple syrup.

Corn and Egg Tortilla (V)

I love corn, especially for breakfast. Try adding a little cumin powder
or smoked paprika with the onions for a Mexican flavour.

SERVES 2

1 tbsp olive oil
1 tbsp finely chopped spring onions
1 tbsp roughly chopped thyme
1 corn cob, kernels removed
2 eggs
2 tbsp crumbled goat's feta
1 cup rocket
2 corn tortillas
2 tbsp tomato chutney or mild
  chilli jam

Heat a frying pan and add the oil, spring onions,
thyme and corn and sauté for about 1 minute until
the corn starts to soften.

In a bowl, whisk the eggs, then add the feta.

Pour the egg mixture into the pan and gently stir
until the egg is almost cooked.

Place half the rocket in the centre of each tortilla,
then top with the egg mixture. Fold the tortilla sides
in to create a parcel. Gently toast in a sandwich press.

Serve with tomato chutney or chilli jam.

Almond and Banana Pancakes (GF, V)

I have used three different flours in this recipe, but you can use only one or two if you like – just have the final quantity equal 2 cups. The fruit provides sweetness, but add ¼ cup grated coconut palm sugar for a little more if you like. Leave out the yoghurt for a dairy-free and vegan alternative.

SERVES 2–4

1 cup besan
½ cup buckwheat flour
½ cup millet flour
½ cup ground almonds
1 tsp low-allergy bicarbonate of soda
1 tsp ground cinnamon
1 banana, mashed
1 apple or pear, grated
3 cups apple or pear juice or soy milk
2 tbsp macadamia, coconut or rice bran oil
blueberries and plain yoghurt mixed with maple syrup, to serve

In a bowl, mix the dry ingredients together, then add the fruit and juice or soy milk. Stir well to combine until the batter is thick and wet. Adjust the consistency by adding more juice or flour if needed.

Heat ½ tablespoon of oil in a frying pan over medium heat, then pour about ½ cup of batter into the pan. Fry until tiny bubbles appear on the surface and the bottom is golden brown, then flip. Cook this side until golden, then transfer to a plate and keep warm. Using a little more oil, repeat with the remaining batter.

Serve the pancakes with fruit, yoghurt and a sweetener if you like.

Congee with Shiitake and Gomashio (DF, GF, V, VG)

This is a common breakfast dish in the East. There are many ways to eat congee, and just as many toppings to have with it. It is very easy to digest and is typically recommended when one is feeling run down, frail or depleted. Gomashio is a Japanese condiment made by grinding sesame seeds and sea salt together. This recipe should be started a day before you plan to serve it.

SERVES 2–4

1 cup organic brown rice
2 cups filtered water or vegetable stock, plus 4 to 5 extra cups
1 cup diced shiitake mushrooms
1 tbsp grated fresh ginger
1 tsp umeboshi vinegar, to serve (optional)

GOMASHIO (OPTIONAL)
½ tsp coarse sea salt
1 tbsp sesame seeds, toasted

Wash and drain the rice a couple of times, then cover with clean water and leave overnight to soak.

The next morning, drain the rice and place in a heavy-based saucepan (a pressure cooker will cut down on cooking time) with the water or stock, mushrooms and ginger. Bring to the boil, reduce the heat to low and simmer for 2 hours. Stir occasionally to prevent sticking. The rice will break down and eventually become like a thick soup. You will probably need to add extra water or stock throughout the cooking process.

For the gomashio, place the salt in a heavy-based saucepan over medium heat. Stir for a minute, or until the smell changes (this is the chlorine burning off). Place the sesame seeds and salt in a mortar and pestle and gently grind, keeping about 70 per cent of the seeds whole.

Serve the congee with the gomashio and vinegar, if using.

Creamy Herbed Mushrooms on Rye Sourdough (DF, V, VG)

For those who like creamy mushrooms, this is for you. It's surprising just how thick a sauce the soy milk creates. Add some diced firm tofu for added protein and use a gluten-free bread if you're avoiding gluten.

SERVES 2

1 tbsp olive oil

2 cups mixed mushrooms (Swiss brown, button, shiitake), cut into quarters

1 garlic clove, chopped

1 tsp sea salt and cracked pepper, or to taste

1 cup soy milk

1 tsp thyme

1 tbsp roughly chopped dill and basil

1 tbsp roughly chopped flat-leaf parsley

2 slices of 100 per cent rye sourdough

Heat a frying pan and add the oil, mushrooms, garlic and salt and pepper. Sauté over medium heat until the mushrooms start to soften, about 1 minute. Then add the milk and thyme. Continue to cook for about 3 minutes, or until almost all the milk has been absorbed, the mushrooms are tender, and the sauce has thickened. Toss the rest of the herbs in just before serving.

Meanwhile, toast the bread, either in a toaster or chargrill pan.

Place the toast on plates and pour over the creamy mushrooms.

Sardines on Toast (DF)

These little fish are so high in calcium, omega 3 and zinc that I have learnt
to love eating them. And they are one of the few fish that are not overfished.
I realise they are a bit strong for some people but do try them like this.
The tahini balances the fishiness and the lemon lifts the whole dish.

SERVES 2

1 tbsp hulled tahini (stir the tahini
before using it as the oil separates)
½ tbsp grated lemon zest
1 tbsp lemon juice
2 tbsp finely chopped flat-leaf parsley
or dill
75 g tin sardines in olive oil, drained
and mashed
2 slices of spelt sourdough

In a bowl, whisk together the tahini, lemon zest and
juice and parsley or dill. Add the sardines and taste for
seasoning. You may like to add a little more lemon juice.

Toast the bread, then spread the sardine mixture
thickly on the two pieces of toast.

Quinoa Porridge (DF, GF, V, VG)

Quinoa is a beautiful gluten-free seed that is super easy to digest and
is especially high in calcium and protein. It's a great alternative to oats
if you're avoiding gluten, and it's so much quicker to cook.

SERVES 2

2½ cups filtered water
1 cup quinoa flakes
1 tbsp grated lemon or orange zest
¼ tsp each ground cinnamon and
ground cardamom
maple syrup, stewed fruit, agave
or grated palm sugar, to sweeten
(optional)
plain yoghurt and/or fruit, to serve
(optional)

In a saucepan, heat the water, then stir in the quinoa
flakes, just as you would do rolled oats. Add the zest and
spices, stir and continue cooking for a minute or two
until the flakes have dissolved.

Sweeten if you like and serve just as it is. Or you may
like to top it with some yoghurt and/or fruit.

The Ultimate Breakfast Smoothie
(DF, GF, V, VG)

A smoothie is one of my favourite ways to start the day. You won't always add all of the options I have listed – these are a guide to the endless possibilities of your magic smoothie. You'll find your favourites and these will change with the seasons. My current favourite is quinoa milk with flaxseed oil, barley grass, LSA, papaya, blueberries, a date and chia seeds.

SERVES 1

BASE

Milk: 1½ cups quinoa, almond, rice, oat, hazelnut or soy milk

Fruit: ½ cup berries, banana, papaya, pear, passionfruit or mango

Sweetener: 1 tsp raw honey, agave, rice syrup or manuka honey

Dried fruit: 1 tbsp pitted dates, sultanas, goji berries, dried cranberries or goldenberries (Incan gooseberries)

Seeds: 1 tsp ground linseeds (flaxseed meal), chia seeds or tahini, hulled (stir the tahini before using it as the oil separates)

Oil: 1 tsp flaxseed, coconut, hazelnut, walnut or brazil nut oil (optional)

Leafy greens: baby spinach, kale, parsley or Asian greens

Micronutrients: 1 tsp spirulina, wheatgrass or barley grass powder

OPTIONAL EXTRAS

1 tsp maca powder
1 tsp LSA
1 tsp acai powder
1 tsp lecithin granules
1 tsp raw cacao powder
1 tsp psyllium husks
1 tsp slippery elm powder

Place the milk in a blender (or in a container and use a hand-held blender), then add the fresh or dried fruit, seeds, oil, micronutrients and sweetener, if using. Now add in whatever extras you like. Process until blended and smooth.

SOUP

I often have soup for dinner, especially in winter. Soups can be just as satisfying as any main meal, especially if you include protein, a grain and veggies. They're also cute in little shot glasses as an aperitif. I like to use quark, soy or almond milk or goat's feta to make a creamy sauce and as I'm obsessed with making my own stocks, soups are a great way to use them.

LEAN GREEN SOUP

MALAY PRAWN HAWKER SOUP

BORSCHT

SMOKED HADDOCK CHOWDER

KOHLRABI SOUP

SPICY PUMPKIN AND PRAWN SOUP

PEASANT SOUP

SEAFOOD GUMBO

FRENCH ONION SOUP

MINESTRONE WITH KALE AND MIXED GRAINS

GREEK FISH STEW

LENTIL AND LEMON SOUP

BOUILLABAISSE

ALMOND SOUP

FAKÉS

WORRIES GO DOWN BETTER WITH SOUP. ~ JEWISH PROVERB

OPPOSITE PAGE: Borscht (top); Spicy Pumpkin and Prawn Soup (bottom)

Lean Green Soup
(DF, GF, R, V, VG)

This soup is perfect on a hot summer night, when you want to eat lightly but still need nourishing. It's raw, so it retains all of the enzymes that are usually destroyed through cooking.

SERVES 2–4

¼ avocado
½ zucchini, chopped
1 cup basil leaves
1 cup baby spinach leaves
1 cup orange juice
1 garlic clove
1 tsp grated fresh ginger
1 tsp coconut palm sugar or panela
1 tsp sea salt or umeboshi vinegar

To Serve
1 tbsp flaxseed oil
½–1 tsp cayenne pepper

Place all the ingredients in a blender and whiz until very smooth. Taste and adjust seasoning if necessary. Finish by swirling in the flaxseed oil and sprinkling on the cayenne.

Malay Prawn Hawker Soup
(DF, GF)

Hawker food means street food, so you'll usually find these basic dishes
are super tasty and simple. (This recipe includes a good technique for making
prawn stock.) Please try to find local prawns, avoiding imported ones.

SERVES 4

500 g green prawns, peeled and
  deveined (keep shells and heads)
1 tbsp rice bran oil or olive oil
1 tsp sea salt
filtered water, to cover
2 cups fish stock
1 tbsp sesame oil
4 garlic cloves, crushed
1 tbsp grated fresh ginger
1 tsp five-spice
20 g vermicelli rice noodles, soaked in
  hot water for about 5 minutes, then
  drained
2 cups bean sprouts, washed and
  drained
1 cup picked fresh crabmeat
  (optional)
4 spring onions, sliced on the
  diagonal
1 small cucumber, deseeded and
  diced
1 long red chilli, thinly sliced

Quickly wash and drain the prawn shells.

Heat the rice bran or olive oil in a wok over high heat
and stir-fry the prawn shells with the salt until the shells
turn pink. Cover generously with the water and simmer
for about 15 minutes until half the liquid has evaporated.

Put the shells and the liquid in a food processor or
blender with the fish stock and blend for a few seconds.
(Or use a hand-held blender and blend in the pan.) Pass
this pulp though a fine sieve and set aside.

In a stockpot or very large saucepan, heat the sesame oil
over medium heat, then add the garlic and ginger and
stir. When the garlic starts to change colour, add the
strained stock and simmer for a few minutes.

Just before serving, add the prawns and five-spice to the
pan and allow the soup to simmer for about 5 minutes.

To serve, divide the noodles among four bowls and
top with the bean sprouts. Ladle the hot soup over the
noodles, making sure that each bowl has some prawns.
Garnish with the crabmeat (if using), spring onions,
cucumber and chilli.

Borscht (GF, V)

You can use all kinds of different root veggies in this soup. Try parsnips
and swedes, and any type of pumpkin. Apple is a nice addition also. The colour
of this soup is magnificent, and it contains heaps of antioxidants and beta carotene,
which will boost your immunity and help your skin to shine. You can avoid peeling
the beetroot and pumpkin if you sieve the soup before serving.
Leave the yoghurt out for a vegan and dairy-free version.

SERVES 4

1 litre vegetable stock
1 red onion, roughly chopped
1 garlic clove, chopped
1 cup roughly chopped pumpkin
4 beetroot with stalks, peeled and
   chopped
1 tsp freshly grated nutmeg
2 tsp umeboshi vinegar or red wine
   vinegar
cracked black pepper
sea salt
½–1 cup plain yoghurt (leave out
   if you're vegan)
4 dill sprigs, to garnish

Put the stock in a stockpot or very large saucepan and bring to the boil. Add the onion, garlic, pumpkin and beetroot and stalks. Put the lid half on the pan and simmer until the veggies are soft, about 20 minutes.

Add the nutmeg, vinegar and pepper to the pan, then, using a hand-held blender, blitz until the soup is smooth. Taste for seasoning and adjust if necessary. You may need to add a little more vinegar and some salt.

Serve with a dollop of yoghurt, a sprig of dill and a bit of pepper.

Smoked Haddock Chowder
(DF, GF)

Whenever I see a fish chowder on a menu, I skip straight over it as I know it will contain cream, milk and a white sauce made with white flour, butter and milk. I'm not going through life without the joys of a creamy chowder though, so here it is – a dairy-free, gluten-free amazing chowder. You can get the smoked fish from delis or fish markets, some fish shops and supermarkets. Alternatively, you can use 500 g clams and make a clam chowder.

SERVES 4

350 g smoked haddock or smoked
   cod fillet (undyed)
1 bay leaf
2 cups filtered water
1 tbsp omega spread or olive oil
1 small onion, finely chopped
1 leek, white part only, halved
   lengthways and thinly sliced
2 celery stalks, thinly sliced
3 potatoes, diced
2 garlic cloves, chopped
2 tsp chopped fresh thyme or ½ tsp
   dried thyme
1 cup soy milk
2 cups fish stock
sea salt (optional)
½ cup chopped flat-leaf parsley
pinch of cayenne pepper (optional)

Place the fish in a deep frying pan with the bay leaf and water. Cover and simmer for 2 minutes. Turn off the heat and leave to stand, covered, for a further 5 minutes. Drain, reserving the liquid, then flake the fish.

Heat the omega spread or oil in a stockpot or very large saucepan over medium heat, then add the vegetables and garlic and fry until softened. Now add the thyme and the reserved cooking liquid and bring to the boil. Reduce the heat to low and simmer for 10 minutes until the vegetables are cooked.

Take out half of the soup and purée, then return to the pan with the flaked fish, the milk and fish stock. Simmer for 3 minutes, taste and add salt if needed.

To serve, sprinkle with the parsley and cayenne pepper (if using).

Kohlrabi Soup
(DF, GF, V, VG)

Kohlrabi is not very well known in Australia. This root veggie tastes like
a cross between cabbage and broccoli, which is no surprise as it is part of
the same cruciferous family. That means it's great for your liver.
This is a lovely creamy soup.

SERVES 2–4

1–2 tbsp olive oil
1 white or brown onion, chopped
500 g kohlrabi, peeled and chopped
2 cups vegetable stock
1 bay leaf
2½ cups soy or almond milk
sea salt and cracked black pepper,
   to taste
½ cup kohlrabi leaves (*see* Note), basil
   or flat-leaf parsley, finely chopped,
   to garnish

Heat the oil in a stockpot or large saucepan over low heat. Add the onion and cook gently until soft, about 2 minutes. Add the kohlrabi and stir to coat. Now add the stock and bay leaf and bring to the boil. Cover with the lid, reduce heat to low and simmer for about 25 minutes, or until the kohlrabi is tender.

Remove the bay leaf from the pan and add the milk. Simmer gently for a few minutes, then blend until smooth. You may want to strain the soup through a fine sieve if the kohlrabi is especially fibrous. Season to taste with salt and pepper.

Garnish with the kohlrabi leaves, basil or parsley and serve in bowls with some crunchy spelt sourdough.

Note: If you're lucky enough to find kohlrabi with its green tops intact, blanch them as you would spinach, then roll the leaves and slice finely, to make a chiffonade. Use as your garnish.

Spicy Pumpkin and Prawn Soup
(DF, GF)

If you'd like to make lots of this soup and freeze it, omit the prawns and basil or kaffir lime leaves, then add these when you're reheating it. This is a really beautiful soup. To make it vegan and vegetarian, omit the fish sauce, shrimp paste and prawns.

SERVES 4

400 g tin coconut milk
4 cups peeled and roughly chopped pumpkin
1 litre fish or vegetable stock
1 tbsp grated coconut palm sugar or panela
1 tsp fish sauce
8 green king prawns, peeled and deveined with tails intact
1 small handful of Thai basil leaves
2 kaffir lime leaves, finely shredded

CURRY PASTE
6 small dried red chillies (the hot ones)
1 tbsp chopped coriander stems and roots
1 tsp coriander seeds, toasted
1 tsp cumin seeds
1 tsp white peppercorns
1 small red onion, diced
1 lemongrass stem, white part only, finely chopped
2 tsp chopped galangal
6 garlic cloves, chopped
2 tsp lime zest
pinch of mace
1 tsp sea salt
1 tsp shrimp paste

For the curry paste, soak the chillies in hot water for about 20 minutes, then drain. Chop finely. In a mortar and pestle, pound the coriander stems and roots, coriander seeds, cumin seeds and peppercorns. Add the remaining ingredients and pound to a fairly smooth paste (you can store the leftover paste in an airtight container in the fridge).

In a stockpot or very large saucepan, heat half the coconut milk over low heat until it starts to thicken. Stir in 1 tablespoon of the curry paste and simmer for a few minutes until fragrant. Now add the pumpkin and stock and simmer for about 20 minutes, until the pumpkin is soft. Cool slightly then purée.

Stir the palm sugar or panela and fish sauce into the soup. Allow the sugar to dissolve before adding the prawns, basil and the rest of the coconut milk. Let the soup simmer until the prawns are pink and the soup is heated through. This will take only about 1 minute. Garnish with the lime leaves and serve.

Peasant Soup (DF, V, VG)

A basic, hearty soup that's perfect for a winter's lunch. Add whatever
vegetables you like – broccoli, corn, capsicum, tomatoes, beans, peas. The barley
makes it a more substantial meal, as does the addition of the pasta.
Leave the barley out for a gluten-free version.

SERVES 4

1 leek, white part only, thinly sliced
2 tbsp olive oil
2 garlic cloves, crushed
1 carrot, diced
2 celery stalks, diced
1 zucchini, diced
½ cup barley, washed
1 tbsp dried thyme
1 bay leaf
1 tsp dried oregano
1 litre fish or vegetable stock
sea salt and cracked black pepper,
   to taste
½ cup brown rice pasta shells
1 cup roughly chopped flat-leaf
   parsley leaves

In a stockpot or very large saucepan, sauté the leek in the oil over medium heat until soft. Add the garlic and cook for another few seconds. Now add the vegetables and stir to coat in the oil. Cook for a few minutes then stir in the barley, herbs and stock.

Bring the soup to the boil, reduce the heat to low and simmer for about 30 minutes, or until the barley is almost cooked. Taste for seasoning. Add the pasta and let it cook to al dente.

Serve garnished with the parsley.

Seafood Gumbo (DF, GF)

This is a substantial and heavenly thing to eat. In the deep south of America, where this dish is popular, they refer to the combination of capsicum, onion and celery as the 'Southern Trinity'. Many southern American dishes start with this combination. Okra is available frozen from supermarkets if you're having trouble finding it. It is such a lovely vegetable but is so underused. Its medicinal uses in treating arthritis and diabetes have been long known.

SERVES 4

500 g okra, chopped
½ cup olive oil
2 tbsp brown rice flour
1 onion, finely diced
2 celery stalks, finely diced
½ green capsicum, diced
1 cup fresh prawn meat
4 garlic cloves, crushed
400 g tin chopped tomatoes
½ cup chopped flat-leaf parsley, plus extra to serve
2 bay leaves
3 spring onions, finely chopped
500 g green prawns, peeled and deveined
500 g picked fresh crabmeat (optional)
2 litres fish stock
sea salt and cracked black pepper, to taste
Tabasco sauce and cayenne pepper, to serve

Sauté the okra in 2 tablespoons of the oil until the strings that keep the okra connected disappear. This will take about 5 minutes. Set aside.

Meanwhile, gently heat another 2 tablespoons of the oil and whisk in the flour. Keep whisking for about 10 minutes until a smooth paste forms and turns a golden colour. Set aside.

In a stockpot or very large flameproof casserole dish over medium heat, sauté the onion, celery and capsicum in the remaining oil until translucent, about 5 minutes. Now add the prawn meat and garlic and cook slowly for another couple of minutes, until the prawns just start to change colour. Add the okra, tomatoes, parsley, bay leaves, spring onions, green prawns, crabmeat (if using) and stock. Simmer for another minute then stir in the flour paste. Simmer gently, stirring frequently so the paste doesn't stick. Season, then garnish with lots of extra parsley.

Serve with the Tabasco sauce and a small bowl of cayenne pepper on the table.

French Onion Soup (V)

There are ways to modernise traditional French food.
Take out the animal stock, cream, butter and white bread and you've
got a healthy take on a classic favourite. Leave the feta
out if you're avoiding dairy.

SERVES 4

2 tbsp olive oil
4 brown onions, thinly sliced
2 garlic cloves, chopped
2 cups dry white wine
1 tbsp fresh thyme leaves or 1 tsp
   dried thyme
2 cups vegetable stock
sea salt and cracked black pepper,
   to taste
2 cups baby spinach
4 thin slices of spelt sourdough bread
   (leave out for gluten-free or use
   gluten-free bread)
1 cup crumbled goat's feta
½ cup chopped flat-leaf parsley

Heat 1 tablespoon of the oil in a large saucepan over medium heat, add the onion and sauté until just starting to brown, about 5 minutes. Stir in the garlic and cook for about 30 seconds. Add the wine and thyme and bring to the boil. Drop back to a simmer for a few minutes. Now pour in the stock and simmer gently for another 20 minutes.

Take four 750 ml ovenproof bowls and place ½ cup of baby spinach in each. Place the bowls on a baking tray, then divide the soup among the bowls. Tear the bread roughly, place it on top of the soup and drizzle with the remaining oil.

Place the tray under a hot grill and cook until the bread is lightly toasted. Remove and sprinkle the feta evenly over the bread. Place the tray back under the grill until the cheese starts to melt.

Serve sprinkled with lots of parsley.

Minestrone with Kale and Mixed Grains (DF, V, VG)

Try using other grains such as millet, amaranth and spelt for different textures, nutrients and flavours. Other veggies like diced zucchini and celery would be lovely in here also. Add 1 cup of whole lentils with the stock for a good hit of protein. This soup freezes well.

SERVES 4

1 onion or leek, diced
2 garlic cloves, finely chopped
½–1 tbsp olive oil
¼ cup each of red, white and black
   quinoa
¼ cup brown rice
¼ cup barley
1 tsp dried oregano
1 bay leaf
400 g tin chopped tomatoes
2 cups vegetable stock
300–500 ml filtered water
1 cup green beans, chopped into
   1-cm pieces
1 carrot, diced
2 cups finely chopped kale

To Serve
1 tbsp fresh oregano, chopped
2 tbsp grated lemon zest (optional)
2 spring onions, finely sliced
   (to garnish)

In a stockpot or very large saucepan, sauté the onion or leek and garlic in the oil over medium heat for about 2 minutes. Add the grains, rice, oregano, bay leaf, tomatoes, stock and water and bring to the boil. Drop to a simmer with the lid half on and continue to cook for about 20 minutes or until the grains are half-cooked. Add the veggies and cook until they are soft, about 15 minutes.

Add the fresh oregano and lemon zest (if using) and serve in a bowl. Garnish with spring onions.

Tip: You can cook the grains separately then scoop them on top of the soup before serving.

Greek Fish Stew (GF)

For something so simple, you'll be surprised just how much flavour
is in this dish. It involves lots of veggies, olive oil, fish and spinach,
so nutritionally wonderful, so exquisitely tasteful.

SERVES 4

1–2 tbsp olive oil
1 onion, chopped
2 garlic cloves, crushed
2 carrots, chopped
1 zucchini, sliced into half-moons
1 desiree or pontiac potato, diced
4 celery stalks, sliced
2 cups thinly sliced green cabbage
1 handful of green beans, cut into
   3-cm pieces
400 g tin whole peeled tomatoes
2 cups vegetable or fish stock
200 g firm, white fish fillet, such as
   flathead, cut into 3-cm pieces
2 cups baby spinach leaves
sea salt and cracked black pepper,
   to taste
4 tbsp crumbled goat's feta
1 tbsp chopped dill

In a stockpot or very large saucepan, heat the oil over
medium heat, then add the onion, garlic, carrot, zucchini,
potato and celery. Sauté gently until the veggies soften.
Next add the cabbage, beans, tomatoes and stock and
bring to the boil. Drop to a simmer for 20 minutes, or
until the veggies are tender.

Add the fish and spinach to the pan and reduce the heat
to low. Cover and simmer for 3 minutes, or until the fish
turns opaque. Taste for seasoning.

Serve sprinkled with the feta and dill.

Lentil and Lemon Soup
(DF, GF, V, VG)

This is one of my favourite things to eat. I feel clean and satisfied during and after the experience. It's green so I know it's great for my liver, as is the lemon; the lentils help to keep my blood sugar even and are a good source of iron, fibre and protein; and I have good oils from the olive oil and pine nuts. Start this recipe a day before by soaking your lentils overnight or use BPA free lentils. Your cooking time will be less and the lentils will be easier to digest. And wait until you taste it. A perfect dish.

SERVES 4

1 onion, thinly sliced
1 tbsp olive oil
1 garlic clove, crushed
1 cup brown or green lentils, soaked
　　overnight
1 litre vegetable stock
6 cups of silverbeet, white stalks
　　removed, or English spinach
1 handful of coriander leaves and
　　stems, roughly chopped
juice of 1 lemon
sea salt and cracked white pepper,
　　to taste
2 tbsp pine nuts, toasted, to serve

TAKLIA
4 garlic cloves, sliced
½ cup olive oil
1 tbsp ground coriander
1 tbsp sea salt

In a stockpot or very large saucepan, sauté the onion in the oil over medium heat until translucent, about 2 minutes. Add the garlic and cook for another few seconds. Now tip in the lentils and stir to coat in the oil. Pour in the stock and simmer until the lentils are soft. This will take about 30 minutes.

Roughly chop the silverbeet or spinach, then add to the pan with the coriander and lemon juice. Stir well, cover the pan with the lid and cook for a few minutes to let the silverbeet or spinach wilt. Purée until smooth. Add more water if the soup is too thick.

For the taklia, fry the garlic in a little of the oil in a frying pan over low heat until it just changes colour – don't let it brown. Put it in a mortar and pestle with the remaining oil, the ground coriander and salt. Pound until it becomes a rough paste.

Divide the soup among four bowls and stir 1 tablespoon of taklia into each. Taste for seasoning. Top with the pine nuts and serve.

Bouillabaisse (DF)

This is definitely one of my favourite dishes. It's light and tasty and it's also one of the few times I cook with tomatoes. Feel free to add other seafood such as scallops or calamari rings. For an easy meal, have the tomato base ready and add the seafood just before serving.

SERVES 4

2 tbsp olive oil
1 onion or leek, diced
4 anchovy fillets
3 garlic cloves, chopped
400 g tin whole peeled tomatoes
1 tbsp tomato paste
2 tsp smoked paprika
1 tsp saffron threads
½ cup dry white wine
2 cups fish stock
1 bay leaf
8 mussels, scrubbed and debearded
8 green prawns, peeled and deveined
  with tails intact
2 x 100 g firm white fish fillets – such
  as blue eye, flathead or kingfish –
  cut into 3-cm pieces
sea salt and cracked black pepper,
  to taste
flat-leaf parsley and lemon wedges,
  to serve

CHARGRILLED BREAD
4 slices of sourdough spelt bread
2 tsp olive oil

Heat a stockpot or very large saucepan over low heat and add the oil. Sauté the onion or leek until translucent.

Meanwhile, make a paste by crushing the anchovies and garlic together, then add this to the pan and continue to sauté for 1 minute over a low heat. Add the tomatoes, tomato paste, paprika, saffron and wine. Allow to simmer for 15–30 minutes until the sauce reduces and thickens a little.

Using a hand-held blender, blitz the sauce to make a smooth purée. Now add the fish stock, bay leaf and mussels, and simmer for 5 or so minutes, until all the mussels open. (Discard any that don't open.)

Add the prawns and fish to the tomato broth and cook for a further few minutes until the fish is opaque and the prawns are turning pink. Season to taste with a little salt and pepper.

Chargrill the bread in a chargrill pan with the oil and a sprinkling of salt.

Ladle the bouillabaisse into shallow bowls, garnish with the parsley and lemon wedges and serve with the chargrilled bread.

Almond Soup (DF, GF, V, VG)

This heavenly, creamy soup is gorgeous served in little shot glasses as an appetiser, or equally lovely served as a starter in a shallow bowl. Depending on the season, serve it chilled or warm. This calcium-filled soup is a hit with the kids also.

SERVES 4–6

1 cup ground almonds
1 litre almond milk (or half milk, half water)
1 leek, white part only, sliced
1 celery heart, diced
cayenne pepper, to taste
2 tbsp flaked almonds
1 tsp freshly grated nutmeg

Place the almonds, milk, leek and celery in a stockpot or large saucepan and simmer until the veggies are soft. Purée, then season with the cayenne pepper and garnish with the flaked almonds and nutmeg.

Fakés (DF, GF, V, VG)

This traditional Greek lentil soup, pronounced *fah-kehs*, has been a favourite thing of mine to eat for many years. That is, I've not made it so much as Greek friends have served it to me. Lucky me, I know. This recipe is pretty close to traditional. The oil and vinegar at the end lift this soup from being yummy to divine. Remember to soak the lentils the day before you plan to serve this soup.

SERVES 4–6

1½ litres vegetable stock
1 litre filtered water
1 cup dried brown or green lentils, soaked overnight and drained
1 large onion, finely diced
1 cup finely diced celery stalks and leaves
1 cup finely diced carrot
½ cup finely diced zucchini
½ red capsicum, finely diced
400 g tin chopped tomatoes
3–4 garlic cloves, crushed
1 cup chopped flat-leaf parsley
2 bay leaves
⅓ cup extra virgin olive oil
1 tsp dried oregano
sea salt (optional)
1 tsp cracked black pepper
2 tbsp balsamic vinegar

Bring the stock and water to a simmer in a stockpot or very large saucepan, then add the lentils and veggies and simmer for 30 minutes. Add the tomatoes, garlic, parsley, bay leaves and pepper. Continue to simmer for another hour, or until the lentils are tender.

Now add the oil and oregano to the pan. Taste for seasoning. You may want a little salt, depending on how salty your stock is. Continue to simmer for a few minutes, then finally stir in the vinegar.

SALADS

Gone are the days when a salad meant boring diet food restricted solely to summer. These days we have all sorts of wonderful ingredients and preparation methods that can turn a simple green salad into an exciting and satisfying main meal. In this chapter you will find recipes that you can put together quickly and make in bulk, plus these salads contain everything you need in a meal. Of course, some may still be a side, it's up to you.

Nothing would be more tiresome than eating and drinking if God had not made them a pleasure as well as a necessity. – Voltaire

Cannellini, Pomegranate and Quinoa Salad (DF, GF, V, VG)

This is a really quick salad to throw together. To make it even yummier, gently warm the oil over low heat, then add 2 cloves of garlic and the sumac. Add this to the dressing, discarding the garlic if you want. Of course other veggies such as steamed broccoli, peas, beetroot or beans will work in this salad, as well as raw capsicum or fennel.

SERVES 4

2 cups quinoa
4 cups filtered water
6 small spears of asparagus, woody
 ends trimmed
400 g tin cannellini beans, drained
 and rinsed
2 corn cobs, kernels removed
1 handful of snow peas, cut into
 three on the diagonal
1 pomegranate, seeds removed
1 cup coriander leaves
1 cup roughly chopped mint leaves
1 cup flat-leaf parsley leaves
2 spring onions, finely chopped
½ cup in total of sesame seeds,
 sunflower seeds and pepitas,
 toasted, plus extra to serve
½ cup walnuts, toasted
2 radishes, thinly sliced
1 handful of chopped coriander,
 to serve

Dressing

½ tbsp umeboshi or white wine vinegar
1 tbsp extra virgin olive oil
 or flaxseed oil
2 tsp sumac, plus extra to serve
grated zest and juice of 1 lemon
grated zest and juice of 1 orange
sea salt and cracked black pepper,
 to taste

Put the quinoa and water in a saucepan and bring to the boil. Drop to a simmer, put the lid half on and cook until you can't see the water and little 'volcano holes' appear in the quinoa. This will take 10–15 minutes. Taste the quinoa; it should be tender and almost cooked. If not, add a splash more water. Put the lid on and turn the heat off. Allow the quinoa to cook in its own steam for another 10 minutes, or until you're ready to serve.

Steam the asparagus until just tender, then rinse under cold water to stop it cooking. When cool enough to handle, cut each spear into thirds.

In a large bowl, toss all the salad ingredients together.

For the dressing, put all the ingredients in a jar and shake well (or whisk in a bowl).

Pour the dressing over the salad and toss again.

Serve on a large platter, sprinkled with the extra sumac and toasted seeds and the chopped coriander.

Smoked Trout, Sweet Potato and Macadamia Salad (DF, GF)

The macadamias and the trout help to make this salad exquisitely rich in good oils. Cashews would work just as well as the macas, and flaxseed oil instead of olive oil in the dressing would also be lovely. Perfect for Autumn.

SERVES 4 AS A STARTER

1 medium sweet potato,
   cut into 3-cm chunks
1 tbsp olive oil
1 tsp each of sea salt and cracked
   black pepper
150 g whole or 2 fillets smoked trout,
   flaked
1 cup whole macadamia nuts, toasted
2 large handfuls of baby spinach
1 cup mint leaves
2 spring onions, thinly sliced

DRESSING
1 tbsp raw honey
¼ cup orange juice
1 tbsp extra virgin olive oil
½ tbsp white balsamic vinegar
1 tsp wholegrain or dijon mustard
½ tsp sea salt
½ tsp cracked white pepper

Preheat the oven to 180°C.

Place the sweet potato on a baking tray, drizzle with the oil and season. Roast in the oven for about 20 minutes, or until golden. Allow to cool slightly.

Place the sweet potato in a bowl, add the flaked trout and the other ingredients and gently toss.

For the dressing, place all the ingredients in a jar and shake well.

Dress and give this beautiful salad a final toss.

Coconut 'Pasta' Salad
(DF, GF)

I've used coconut strips in this salad instead of pasta. It's not the same
as pasta of course, as you will experience no bloating, heaviness or spikes
in your blood sugar. And it's completely moreish.

SERVES 4

2 zucchini
1 carrot
1 red capsicum
1 yellow capsicum
1 fresh young coconut or 2 cups
  shredded coconut
1 tbsp arame, soaked in 2 tbsp water
  for a few minutes until soft then
  drained (reserve liquid)
1 tsp cayenne pepper
3 tbsp lime juice
grated zest of 1 lime
1 tsp fish sauce (or ½–1 tsp sea salt if
  you want it vego and vegan)

Using a mandoline if you have one, finely shred the
zucchini, carrot and capsicums.

If you have a special tool to shred coconut, then use this
to create strips, otherwise use shredded coconut in a
packet.

Place the veggies in a bowl, add the remaining
ingredients, toss well and marinate for about 30 minutes
before serving. If you need moisture and/or salt, add the
arame liquid to taste.

Roast Jerusalem Artichoke Salad with Almonds and Pomegranate Dressing (DF, GF, V, VG)

Jerusalem artichokes are known to stabilise blood sugar, so they are great for those with sugar cravings and anyone wanting to boost their fibre intake. Pomegranate dressing is available from good delis and grocers.

SERVES 2–4

2 large handfuls of Jerusalem artichokes
1 garlic bulb, unpeeled and broken into cloves
2 tbsp olive oil
1 tsp sea salt
1½ cups whole almonds, toasted
1 cup mint leaves

DRESSING
1 tsp pomegranate molasses
1 tbsp red wine vinegar
3 tbsp extra virgin olive oil
1 French shallot, thinly sliced
1 garlic clove, crushed
pinch of sea salt

Preheat the oven to 180°C.

Give the artichokes a good scrub with a veggie brush or a clean, damp cloth. Trim to remove any black bits and rinse. Place on a baking tray with the garlic, then drizzle with the oil and season with the salt. Bake for 20–30 minutes, or until tender.

Allow the artichokes to cool slightly, then place in a bowl with the almonds and mint.

For the dressing, mix all the ingredients together in a small bowl.

Drizzle the dressing over the still-warm salad and serve immediately, or in a day or two, when it will be just as good.

Japanese Sweet Potato and Pickled Ginger Salad (DF, GF, V, VG)

The basil combined with the pickled ginger gives this salad a unique flavour.
It looks great and is wonderful for your digestion, thanks to the bitter flavour
of the rocket and the anti-inflammatory effect of the ginger. You could use the recipe
for Pickled Ginger (*see* page 170) or buy some without added colouring.

SERVES 4

2 tbsp safflower oil
1 large sweet potato, unpeeled
   and cut into 2-cm thick slices
1 cucumber, thinly sliced on the
   diagonal
1 red onion, thinly sliced
   (use a mandoline if you have one)
2 cups rocket
½ cup pickled ginger

DRESSING
2 garlic cloves
¼ cup chopped basil leaves
juice of 2 limes
1 tbsp white wine vinegar
2 tbsp tamari
1 tbsp grated coconut palm sugar
2 spring onions, chopped
½ cup safflower oil or rice bran oil
½ tsp sesame oil
½ tsp cracked white pepper

For the dressing, place all the ingredients in a food
processor and blitz until smooth. Set aside.

Heat the oil in a frying pan over medium heat and cook
the sweet potato in batches until golden on both sides.
Keep it quite firm but not crunchy. Drain on paper
towels.

In a bowl, combine the cucumber, onion, rocket and
pickled ginger, pour on the dressing and toss well.

To serve, overlap the sweet potatoes in a line or circle
on a large plate, then top with the salad.

Warm Roasted Beetroot and Almond Salad (DF, GF, V, VG)

I wrote the recipe for this salad for a *Good Chef Bad Chef* episode on roasting, then realised that this salad is deserving of a stand-alone place in this book. It's so rich in colour, flavour and nutrients that once you've made it, it'll quickly become a favourite.

SERVES 2

4 small beetroot
1 red onion, quartered
2 tsp olive oil
1 red onion, quartered
½ tsp sea salt
½ cup whole almonds, toasted
1 cup shredded radicchio

DRESSING
1 tbsp maple syrup
1 tsp red wine vinegar
1 tsp sumac
1 tbsp olive oil
½ tsp each of sea salt and cracked
   black pepper

Preheat the oven to 180°C.

Scrub the beetroot with a veggie brush or a clean cloth. Place on a sheet of greased foil, then fold in the sides and seal. Transfer to a baking tray.

On the same tray, drizzle the onion with the oil and sprinkle on a little salt. Bake for about 30 minutes, or until the beetroot are tender and the onion is golden. (Test the beetroot with a skewer.)

For the dressing, mix all the ingredients in a bowl. Set aside.

When cool enough to handle, cut up the beetroot and place in a bowl with the onion, almonds and radicchio. Drizzle with the dressing and gently toss.

Som Tam (DF, GF)

Definitely in my top 10 favourite things to eat. This salad, made
from green papaya (and sometimes green mango), has all the elements
of a good Asian dish – sweet, salty, sour and spicy. Dried shrimp are
available from Asian grocery stores.

SERVES 4

1 green papaya or mango
¼ cup peanuts
1–2 bird's eye chillies, chopped
2 garlic cloves, chopped
2 tbsp dried shrimp
1 tbsp grated coconut palm sugar
1 tomato, cut into wedges
1 tbsp fish sauce
2 tbsp lime juice
½ cup coriander leaves
1 cup bean sprouts
cooked organic brown rice, to serve

Peel, seed and shred the papaya using a mandoline or
grater or by hand. If using mango, peel then finely slice
the flesh. Set aside.

To make the dressing, use a mortar and pestle to lightly
pound the peanuts, chilli, garlic and dried shrimp (or
blitz them in a food processor). Add the palm sugar,
tomato, fish sauce and lime juice and pound gently
or process briefly to combine.

Toss the dressing with the papaya or mango, coriander
and sprouts and serve with a bowl of brown rice.

Roast Veggie Salad with Butter Beans and Tahini and Cumin Dressing (GF, V)

A variation of this is probably my most regular lunch. Sometimes I add cooked quinoa or barley; add coriander or basil to the tahini dressing; sprinkle with toasted seeds and nuts; and vary the veggies depending on the season. Keep the skin on all your veggies except the onions, but be sure to give them a good scrub with a veggie brush, if you have one.

SERVES 4

1 red onion, quartered
1 cup unpeeled and roughly chopped Japanese pumpkin
1 cup unpeeled, chopped sweet potato
1 cup whole button mushrooms
4 beetroot, scrubbed clean
2 carrots, chopped
2 tbsp olive oil
4 garlic cloves, unpeeled
1 tsp each sea salt and cracked black pepper
1 tbsp thyme or rosemary leaves
400 g tin butter beans or navy beans, drained and rinsed
2 handfuls of baby spinach or rocket
1 tbsp grated lemon or lime zest
2 spring onions, finely chopped
1 tsp extra virgin olive oil
1 tsp balsamic, umeboshi or white wine vinegar
2 lemon cheeks, to serve

TAHINI AND CUMIN DRESSING

1 cup plain yoghurt (leave out if you're dairy free or vegan)
2 tbsp hulled tahini (stir the tahini before using it as the oil separates)
1 tsp ground cumin
1 garlic clove, chopped with a pinch of salt
juice of 1 lemon
pinch of cracked white pepper

Preheat the oven to 180–200°C.

In a roasting tin, combine the onion, pumpkin, sweet potato, mushrooms, beetroot and carrot with the olive oil, garlic, salt, pepper and thyme or rosemary and mix well. Roast, turning once, for 30–40 minutes, or until the veggies are tender and golden. Let cool slightly.

In a mixing bowl, combine the veggies with the butter or navy beans, leafy greens, lemon or lime zest and spring onions. Dress with a little olive oil and the vinegar.

For the tahini dressing, whisk all the ingredients together until the consistency of thickened cream. You may need to add a little water. Taste and adjust seasoning.

Serve the warm salad with dollops of tahini dressing and garnish with the lemon cheeks.

Prawn and Lychee Salad (DF, GF)

In summer when the days and nights are long and warm, this is a perfect
lunch or starter for dinner. Summer means stone fruit, and here's a
great way to use the delightful lychee.

SERVES 4

1 red capsicum
500 g cooked large prawns, peeled
  and deveined
2 lemongrass stems
1 handful watercress, sunflower
  sprouts or rocket, roughly torn
1 handful Vietnamese mint,
  roughly torn
2 cups peeled and deseeded lychees
2 kaffir lime leaves, thinly sliced

DRESSING

1 tbsp rice wine vinegar
1 tbsp lime juice
1 tbsp fish sauce (leave out if you're
  vego or vegan)
1 tbsp grated fresh ginger
1 tbsp grated coconut palm sugar
  or panela
1 tsp dried chilli flakes
1 tbsp thinly sliced spring onions
2 tablespoons sliced French shallots

For the dressing, place all the ingredients in a jar
and shake. Set aside.

Cut the capsicum in half, take out the seeds and white
bits, slice into long, thin strips and put in a bowl.

Halve the prawns lengthways and add them to the
capsicum in the bowl.

Take the lemongrass and cut off the tough green ends
and outer layers. Bruise the tender white part with
the side of your knife and heel of your hand, then
thinly slice. Add to the bowl along with the watercress,
sunflower sprouts or rocket and mint.

Tear the lychees in half and add to the bowl also.

Lastly, throw the lime leaves into the salad, pour the
dressing over the top and toss. Chill until ready to serve.

Kerabu (DF, GF)

Kerabu is a refreshing Malaysian side dish that goes well with dark, highly spiced dishes such as curries. Scald the bean sprouts, if you wish, by running boiling water through them in a sieve. Quickly follow with cold water to keep them crisp. Leave the dried shrimp and fish sauce out if you'd like this dish vego or vegan.

SERVES 4

1 cup desiccated coconut
2 tbsp dried shrimp
1 cup trimmed bean sprouts
1 cup thinly sliced cucumber
1 handful of green beans, sliced on the diagonal
1 handful of snow peas, sliced on the diagonal
1 cup thinly sliced wombok (Chinese cabbage)
1 cup julienned carrot
4 spring onions, thinly sliced
1 handful of Vietnamese mint, thinly sliced
6 long red chillies, thinly sliced (less if you like)
2 tbsp lime juice (more if you like)
1 tbsp fish sauce, or to taste
1 tsp grated coconut palm sugar or panela, or to taste

Dry-roast the coconut in a heavy-based frying pan until light brown and aromatic, then either pound it in a mortar and pestle or blitz in a food processor until it resembles breadcrumbs. (Alternatively, you can use fresh coconut, and omit the roasting.)

Rinse the dried shrimp, drain, dry with paper towel and grind coarsely, either in a mortar and pestle or a food processor.

In a large bowl, combine the coconut, shrimp, vegetables, mint and chilli.

In a small bowl, mix the lime juice, fish sauce and palm sugar or panela to taste, then toss with the salad.

Sweet Roast Pumpkin with Walnuts and Cannellini Beans (DF, GF, V, VG)

This dish is a good example of how yummy and healthy a vegan diet can be.
You have your protein and fibre from the legumes, omega 3 from the walnuts,
omega 9 in the olive oil, antioxidants from the pumpkin and the rosemary
(it's also a lovely herb for the liver).

SERVES 2

200 g pumpkin, unpeeled and cut
    into 3-cm chunks (to yield 2 cups)
1 tbsp olive oil
1 tsp sea salt
1 tbsp maple syrup
1 cup walnut pieces, toasted
400 g tin cannellini beans, drained
    and rinsed
1 tbsp roughly chopped rosemary

Preheat the oven to 180°C.

Place the pumpkin on a baking tray and sprinkle on the oil, salt and maple syrup. Bake for about 20 minutes, or until the pumpkin starts to become golden.

About 5 minutes before the pumpkin is ready, toss the walnuts in with the pumpkin and roast until a golden colour. Allow to cool a little.

Place the pumpkin and walnuts in a large bowl and gently toss with the cannellini beans and rosemary.

SEAFOOD

Seafood is full of good protein and omega 3 oils, both of which are essential to good health. Seafood itself doesn't contain omega 3s, rather it's the algae that it eats. If you are mindful when choosing your seafood, ensuring it has been sustainably caught, is local and is not at the top of the food chain (these types of fish contain dangerously high levels of heavy metals), then it can be part of your diet. The Australian Conservation Society has a good app to help you make informed decisions about buying seafood.

Guilt-free Crumbed Fish and Chips
Chermoula Kingfish with Quinoa Pilaf
    and Tahini and Yoghurt Sauce
Steamed Blue Eye with Noodles
Seafood Paella
Malay Tempeh Noodles
Herbed Herrings and Mash
Salmon with Dried Figs and Caperberries
Scallop Ravioli in a Light Tomato Broth
Seafood Lasagne
Italian Mackerel in a Paper Bag with Freekeh
Balinese Seafood Skewers
Seafood Balls with Green Curry Sauce
Thai Fried Rice
Nurturing Asian Mussels
Poached Fish with Orange and Sesame Sauce
Whole Sardines Stuffed with Quinoa and Goji Berries
Prawns, Mussels and Clams in a Paper Bag
Honey Soy Salmon with Buckwheat Noodles

Give a man a fish and you feed him for a day. Teach a man to fish and you feed him for a lifetime. – Chinese Proverb

Guilt-free Crumbed Fish and Chips (DF, GF)

If the fish you get is quite thick, you may need to pop it in the oven for
5 minutes to finish off the cooking. You can always skip the eggs and crumbs
and simply flour the fish for a lighter option. But sometimes, as I'm sure
you'll agree, it's nice to have it crumbed.

SERVES 2

CHIPS
4 kipfler potatoes
4 garlic cloves, unpeeled
1–2 tbsp olive oil
2 tsp sea salt
cracked black pepper

FISH
2 eggs
½ cup rice crumbs
½ cup brown rice flour
2 x 150 g firm white fish fillets
   (such as wild barramundi, kingfish,
   red emperor or blue eye), skin off
2 tbsp olive oil
½ tsp sea salt
good-quality soy mayonnaise or
   Tahini Tartare (*see* page 148),
   to serve

Preheat your oven to 200°C.

For the chips, scrub clean the spuds, then chop them
into small chunks on the diagonal. Place them on a
baking tray with the garlic and coat with the oil and
seasoning. Bake for 20 or so minutes, or until golden.

Meanwhile, for the fish, whisk the eggs in a large,
shallow bowl and season. Place the rice crumbs in a
similar bowl and the flour in a third bowl. Coat your
fish in the flour – shaking off any excess– then dip in
the egg and then finally coat in the crumbs.

Just before you take the potatoes out of the oven, cook
the fish. Heat the oil in a frying pan over a high heat,
add the fish, and cook until golden, about 2 minutes
depending on the thickness, then flip. Cook for another
2 minutes. Season, then drain on paper towel. To test if
the fish is cooked, run a small, sharp knife through the
thickest part. It should go all the way through and the
flesh should look opaque.

Serve the fish with the chips and a dollop of soy mayo
or tartare sauce on the side.

Chermoula Kingfish with Quinoa Pilaf and Tahini and Yoghurt Sauce (GF)

I sometimes make this dish with mushrooms instead of fish. Then it will be gluten free and vegetarian. In this case, leave out the chermoula. Place 8 whole portobello mushrooms in a large heavy-based pan with a little olive oil. Season and cook over very low heat for about 20 minutes, turning to cook on both sides. Serve with the Quinoa Pilaf and Tahini and Yoghurt Sauce, unless you're dairy free. In that case omit the yoghurt.

SERVES 4

4 x 150 g kingfish fillets, skin on
1 tsp sea salt, or to taste (optional)
1 tbsp olive oil or rice bran oil
flat-leaf parsley or coriander leaves,
    to serve

Chermoula
½ red onion
4 garlic cloves, peeled
2 handfuls each of coriander and
    parsley, roughly chopped
1 cup olive oil
1 tbsp ground cumin
1 tbsp grated fresh or ground
    turmeric
1 tbsp sweet paprika
2 tsp ground ginger
½–¾ cup lemon juice, or to taste

Quinoa Pilaf
1 white onion, diced
1 tbsp olive oil
1 garlic clove, crushed
2 tsp ground cumin
1 cinnamon stick
4 cardamom pods, seeds ground
1 tsp grated fresh turmeric
⅓ cup roughly chopped whole
    almonds
1 cup quinoa
2 tbsp millet
2 cups water
1 tsp sea salt
1 kaffir lime leaf, thinly sliced

Tahini and Yoghurt Sauce
1 cup plain yoghurt
½ cup hulled tahini (stir the tahini
    before using it as the oil separates)
1 cup chopped coriander leaves
    and stems
1 garlic clove, chopped with 1 tsp
    of salt
zest and juice of 1 lemon
pinch of cracked white pepper
2 tbsp olive oil

For the chermoula, place the onion and garlic in a food processor and process until just combined. Add the herbs and continue to process with a little of the oil. Add the spices and blitz again until combined. Finally, pour in the lemon juice and enough of the remaining oil and blitz to make a smooth paste. Taste and add more lemon juice if needed.

Rub the chermoula all over both sides of the fish fillets and season with a little salt (if using). Put in the fridge to marinate while you prepare the pilaf and tahini dressing.

For the pilaf, in a large saucepan sauté the onion in the oil over medium heat until translucent, about 2 minutes. Add the garlic and cook for another minute or so until fragrant. Now stir in the spices and almonds and keep stirring. The spices may stick a little. Pour in the quinoa and millet and toast by stirring for a minute or so in the oil and spices. Add the water, salt and kaffir lime leaf and bring to the boil. Reduce the heat to low and, with the lid half on, simmer for about 20 minutes, or until the quinoa and millet are almost cooked. Turn the heat off, cover with the lid and let the pilaf continue to cook in the residual heat in the pan. Don't let it go mushy; the grains should be separate and still have a little bite.

For the tahini and yoghurt sauce, whisk all the ingredients together (or use a hand-held blender) until the dressing is the consistency of pouring cream. You may need to add a little water or more lemon juice.

Pan-fry the kingfish in the oil in a hot frying pan over high heat, skin side first. Allow the skin to become crunchy—this should take about 2 minutes depending on the thickness of the fillets. Flip, then cook on the other side for about 1 minute. Remove from the pan and drain on paper towel.

For each serving, tightly pack a cup with the pilaf and carefully empty it by turning the cup upside down on a serving plate. Place a fish fillet next to it and a dollop of tahini and yoghurt sauce on the side, or smear about 2 tablespoons of the sauce across the plate. Garnish with the parsley or coriander and serve.

Steamed Blue Eye
with Noodles (DF, GF)

Steaming is a nutritious and quick way to cook. If you don't have a bamboo
or other steamer, pour water to a depth of a few centimetres into a frying pan,
place all the ingredients in a shallow bowl, transfer to the pan and cover with a lid.
Try to get 100 per cent quinoa or buckwheat noodles so that the
dish remains gluten free.

SERVES 2

2 x 150 g firm white fish fillets
   (such as blue eye, wild barramundi
   or flathead)
½ cup water
1 tbsp shaoxing rice wine or dry
   sherry
1–2 tbsp tamari
1 tsp sesame oil
1 tbsp julienned fresh ginger
2 spring onions, julienned
½ cup wood ear fungus
2 bok choy, halved lengthways
125 g quinoa noodles, cooked
½ cup coriander leaves
1 tsp cracked white pepper

Cut the fish into big chunks and place in a shallow bowl
that will fit inside your bamboo steamer. Place the bowl
inside the steamer and transfer to a wok or pan half full
of boiling water. Pour the water, wine or sherry, tamari
and sesame oil over the fish and scatter on the ginger,
half the spring onions and the wood ear. Cover and
steam for 5–6 minutes.

A few minutes before the fish is ready, place the bok
choy on top of the fish. Cover again and steam for a
further minute until the bok choy has softened and the
fish is cooked. The flesh should break away easily when
prodded with a fork.

To serve, divide the noodles between two large soup
plates. Top with the fish and the bok choy. Gently pour
the liquid from the steamer bowl over the fish. Garnish
with the rest of the spring onions, the coriander leaves
and pepper.

Seafood Paella (DF, GF)

You'll need a big pan for this dish, preferably a paella pan. You can use any heavy-based large, flat pan, however. This is a pretty spectacular dish as it is, but try adding peas (if using fresh peas, add with the crab claw; if using frozen ones, add with the rest of the seafood).

SERVES 4

TOMATO SAUCE
1 onion, diced
½ red capsicum, roughly diced
2 tbsp olive oil
2 garlic cloves, crushed
400 g tin crushed tomatoes
1 tbsp tomato paste
2 cups fish stock
pinch of saffron threads
1 bay leaf
sea salt

PAELLA
1 onion, diced
2 tbsp olive oil
2 garlic cloves, crushed
2 tbsp finely chopped coriander stems
2 anchovy fillets
1 cup organic short-grain brown rice
4 crab claws
8 green prawns, peeled and deveined
　with tails intact
8 mussels, scrubbed and debearded
1 x 200 g firm white fish fillet
　(such as blue eye or flathead),
　cut into 3-cm chunks
flat-leaf parsley leaves and lemon
　wedges, to serve

For the tomato sauce, sauté the onion and capsicum in the oil in a saucepan over medium heat until the onion is translucent, about 2 minutes. Add the garlic and stir for another minute. Add the tomatoes, tomato paste, stock, saffron, bay leaf and seasoning. Stir and simmer for 10–15 minutes. Remove the bay leaf, then blend. Taste for seasoning and adjust if necessary. Note: don't oversalt at this stage as the anchovies will add extra salt later. Set aside.

For the paella, sauté the onion in the oil in a paella pan or large heavy-based frying pan over medium heat until translucent. Add the garlic, coriander stems and anchovies. Sauté for another minute. Now tip in the rice and let it toast in the oil for a minute or two, stirring continuously. This is an important process as it coats the wholegrain rice in oil, which helps to form the paella's crust. Add the reserved tomato sauce and crab claws. Gently simmer until the rice is almost cooked, about 20 minutes. A golden crust should form on the bottom of the pan. Place the seafood on top and simmer gently for another minute or so, or until the seafood is cooked. Discard any mussels that don't open. Scatter on the parsley and serve with the lemon wedges.

Malay Tempeh Noodles (DF, GF)

There are a few steps to this dish, but once you have all the components prepared, it's just a matter of tossing it all together – like a stir-fry. It's worth the little bit of effort it takes for a lot of reward. This dish will be gluten free if you use 100 per cent quinoa or buckwheat noodles. And leaving out the eggs won't detract from its gorgeousness.

SERVES 2

2 tbsp tamari
1 cup cubed tempeh
1 potato, cubed (optional)
7–8 tbsp rice bran oil or grapeseed oil
6 green prawns, peeled and deveined
2 French shallots, thinly sliced
2 garlic cloves, crushed
1 tbsp grated fresh ginger
3 cups chopped veggies (such as snow peas, carrot, red capsicum, cabbage)
125 g quinoa or buckwheat noodles, cooked
2 eggs
1 cup mung bean sprouts
1 tbsp lime juice

SAUCE
4 tbsp tamari
4 tbsp kecap manis
¼ cup good-quality tomato sauce

CHILLI PASTE
12 dried red chillies, soaked in water until softened a little
2 tbsp rice bran oil or grapeseed oil
1 tbsp curry powder
2 tbsp filtered water

TO SERVE
1 lime, quartered
1 cup coriander leaves
1 tbsp spring onions, green part only, finely chopped
2 long red chillies, finely chopped

In a small bowl, pour the tamari over the tempeh and let it marinate for a few minutes.

For the sauce, mix together all the ingredients and set aside.

For the chilli paste, drain the chillies, then purée in a blender. Add the curry powder, oil and a splash or two of water, as needed. Heat a wok and stir-fry the paste over high heat until the oil splits and rises to the surface. Put the paste in a bowl and set aside. The excess paste can be stored in the fridge for up to a week.

Boil or steam the potato (if using) until tender. Set aside. Heat the wok again and add 3 tablespoons of the oil. Drain the tempeh (reserve the tamari for later use) and fry the tempeh in the oil until golden on both sides. Drain on paper towel, then set aside.

To the same wok (you may need a little more oil), add the prawns and stir-fry quickly until just pink. Remove and set aside.

Heat the wok again and add 2 tablespoons of the oil. Throw in the shallots, garlic and ginger and toss for a few seconds, then add 3 tablespoons of the chilli paste. Stir-fry for a minute or so, then add the veggies including the potato. It will start to smell really nice now. Add the noodles and toss to combine. Return the prawns and tempeh to the wok and stir-fry for another minute or so. Add the sauce and stir through.

Create a well in the centre of the wok by pushing everything up along the side. Add 2 teaspoons of oil, then crack in the eggs. Quickly scramble them and mix in with the other ingredients.

Take the wok off the heat, add the sprouts and lime juice and toss until combined. Garnish with the lime wedges, coriander, spring onion and chilli and serve.

Herbed Herrings and Mash (DF, GF)

Make sure the herrings you buy are wild, not farmed. If you can't get
herrings, then wild sardines are just as lovely. This is an adaptation
of a traditional Swedish dish.

SERVES 2

2 tbsp chopped dill
2 tbsp chopped flat-leaf parsley
8 x 80–100 g large herring or sardine
   fillets, skin on
sea salt and cracked black pepper
2 tbsp brown rice flour or besan
2 tbsp olive oil

MASH

2 potatoes, peeled and chopped
1 tbsp olive oil
sea salt and cracked black pepper,
   to taste

TO SERVE

flat-leaf parsley sprigs, fried in
   olive oil until crisp, then drained
   (optional)
1 lemon, quartered

For the mash, cook the potatoes in salted boiling water
until tender, then drain. (Or you can steam them.) Mash
in the pan with the olive oil and seasoning. Keep warm.

Meanwhile, place the herbs on a plate, then press both
sides of each fish fillet into the herbs. Press together two
fillets, skin side out, so you have four 'sandwiches'.

Season the flour, then dust each 'flounder' with the
seasoned flour. Do the same with the herrings, if using.

Heat the oil in a large frying pan, add the fish, skin
side down, and fry until golden on both sides. Don't
overcook. They will take about 1 minute on each side.
Drain on paper towel.

Place the fish in a clock-like pattern around a large plate
and dollop the mash in the centre. Garnish with the
fried parsley (if using) and lemon wedges and serve.

Salmon with Dried Figs and Caperberries (DF, GF)

You can use any fish here and even prawn or tofu would be lovely. Of course, check the sustainability of the fish first. The pomegranate molasses makes this dish sweet and sour at the same time, and the caperberries create the saltiness.

SERVES 4

2½ tbsp rice bran oil
sea salt and cracked white pepper
4 x 150 g wild salmon fillets, skin on
2 red Asian shallots, thinly sliced
½ cup Iranian dried figs, halved
1 tbsp caperberries
½ cup dry white wine
2 cups fish or vegetable stock
½ tbsp pomegranate molasses
1 tbsp thyme leaves
sea salt
½ cup flat-leaf parsley leaves

Pour 2 tablespoons of the oil into a very hot cast-iron or non-stick frying pan over a high heat. Season the fish on both sides and place in the pan, skin side down. Cook for 1 minute, turn and cook for another minute. The salmon will be deep pink in the centre. Depending on how well you like your salmon cooked, you may want to cook it for a little longer. Drain on paper towel.

Add the shallot and the remaining oil to the same pan and sauté over medium heat until softened and just changing colour. Stir in the figs, caperberries and wine. Bring up to a gentle simmer and allow the alcohol to evaporate. Add the stock, pomegranate molasses and thyme and reduce the liquid slightly. Return the fish to the pan and simmer just until the fish is heated through. Taste for seasoning.

Sprinkle with the parsley and serve at the table in the pan.

Scallop Ravioli in a Light Tomato Broth (DF)

I don't eat pasta often, which is why there aren't many recipes in my books on how to make it. This is an exception though, being a really light and totally easy recipe. Spelt flour is heavier than the refined white flour usually used to make pasta, but it won't leave you feeling heavy. It will take a little longer to cook than regular pasta but it will be quicker to digest.

SERVES 2

Tomato Broth
½ onion, chopped
2 tbsp olive oil
2 garlic cloves, crushed
400 g tin crushed tomatoes
1 tbsp tomato paste
2 cups fish stock
½ cup dry white wine
pinch of saffron threads
1 tbsp fresh thyme leaves or
    1 tsp dried thyme
1 bay leaf
sea salt

Ravioli Filling
8 large scallops, no roe
2 garlic cloves, crushed
1 tbsp olive oil
1 tbsp shredded fresh basil
pinch of sea salt

Ravioli
2½ cups spelt flour, sifted,
    plus extra for dusting
1 tsp sea salt
3 eggs
olive oil

To Serve
1 tbsp shredded basil
cracked white or black pepper

For the tomato broth, sauté the onion in the oil in a saucepan over medium heat until translucent, about 2 minutes. Add the garlic and stir for another minute. Add the tomatoes, tomato paste, stock, wine, saffron, thyme, bay leaf and seasoning. Stir and simmer for about 20 minutes, then blend. Strain into the pan, then put back on a very low simmer until the pasta is ready.

For the ravioli filling, place all the ingredients in a bowl and gently stir. Leave in the fridge while you prepare your pasta.

For the ravioli, place the flour and salt in a bowl. Lightly beat two of the eggs and whisk into the seasoned flour. Using your hands, form the dough into a ball and knead on a lightly floured surface for 10 minutes until you have a bouncy, smooth ball. Put back in the bowl and cover with a clean tea towel. Let it sit for about 30 minutes. (You can do this in a food processor if you like. Simply add the flour, salt and then the eggs. Process for 2 minutes or until a ball forms. Give it a quick knead on a floured board, then cover in a bowl.)

Put a large saucepan of water on to boil.

Roll the dough out very thinly, about 2-mm thick. Using a 10-cm round cutter, press out 16 rounds from the dough. Place a scallop and some of the filling in the centre of eight of the rounds. Set the other rounds aside. Lightly beat the remaining egg. Brush the edge of each filled round with a little egg, cover with one of the reserved rounds and press around the edge to seal.

Carefully drop the ravioli in the simmering water for a couple of minutes until the pasta looks cooked. Test by squeezing one edge between your thumb nail and middle finger to make sure it is al dente. Take out with a slotted spoon and allow excess liquid to drain away.

Gently divide the ravioli between two shallow bowls and ladle 1 cup of hot tomato broth over the top. Garnish with the basil and pepper and serve.

Seafood Lasagne (DF, GF)

I mentioned the joys of this dish in my last book, *Eating For The Seasons*,
as a variation on the Vegetarian Lasagne. I've had many people request
the recipe – so here it is. Seriously heavenly.

SERVES 4

NAPOLI SAUCE

1 onion, diced

2 tbsp olive oil

2 garlic cloves, crushed

2 anchovy fillets

2 x 400 g tins chopped tomatoes
   or a 700 g bottle of passata

1 tbsp tomato paste

1 bay leaf

1 tsp each sea salt and cracked pepper,
   or to taste

WHITE SAUCE

2 tbsp omega spread or olive oil

½ cup brown rice flour

2 cups soy milk

1 tsp sea salt, or to taste

SEAFOOD

4 anchovy fillets, chopped

4 garlic cloves, chopped

1 tbsp olive oil

4 green large prawns, peeled,
   deveined and cut in half widthways

1 x 200 g flathead or wahoo fillet,
   cut into 3-cm squares

4 large scallops, no roe, cut in half
   widthways

12 gluten-free lasagne sheets

¼ cup each of chopped basil and
   flat-leaf parsley

cracked black pepper

1 tbsp olive oil, extra

For the napoli sauce, sauté the onion in the oil in a saucepan over medium heat for 1 minute, then add the garlic and anchovies and sauté for another minute. Stir in the rest of the ingredients and simmer for 5–10 minutes, or until the sauce has thickened a little. Set aside.

For the white sauce, heat the omega spread or oil in a saucepan over medium heat, then gradually add the flour, stirring continuously. When a smooth paste forms, slowly pour in the milk, and keep stirring to prevent lumps from forming. Season and stir for another minute or so until the sauce thickens. Set aside.

Preheat the oven to 180°C.

For the seafood, make a paste by mixing the anchovies and garlic with the oil. Place the prawns, fish and scallops in a bowl and rub the paste all over the seafood. Season.

To assemble, spoon a quarter of the napoli sauce into the base of an ovenproof baking dish, approximately 30 x 20 cm. Follow with a layer of the lasagne sheets, top with the fish and a third of the white sauce and sprinkle on a third of the herbs. Add another layer of lasagne sheets, a third of the remaining napoli sauce and cover with the prawns and half the remaining white sauce and herbs. Add another layer of lasagne sheets, the scallops, half the remaining napoli sauce, some pepper and the remaining herbs. Finish with a layer of lasagne sheets, napoli sauce and white sauce. Drizzle with the oil. Bake for 30–40 minutes, or until the lasagne sheets are cooked. Test by piercing with a knife.

Italian Mackerel in a Paper Bag with Freekeh (DF)

Freekeh is a young wheat grain that has been smoked over barley.
It contains gluten but most people find it easier to digest than regular
wheat grain. If you'd prefer to not eat any gluten, then use quinoa instead.

SERVES 4

1 cup cracked freekeh or quinoa,
  cooked until al dente
1 red Asian shallot, finely diced
1 lemon, thinly sliced
2 x 200 g wild mackerel fillets, cut
  in half, skin off
2 tsp capers, rinsed and squeezed dry
2 tomatoes, diced
8 black olives, pitted and halved
1 handful of basil leaves
1 tbsp julienned preserved lemon
  or grated zest of 1 lemon
1–2 garlic cloves, crushed
cracked white or black pepper
½ cup chargrilled capsicum, cut
  into thin strips (optional)
2 tsp olive oil

Preheat the oven to 180°C. Prepare four pieces of baking paper about 30 cm square.

In a bowl, mix the freekeh with the shallot.

Lay the sheets of paper on a bench and place a few slices of lemon in the centre of each piece. Divide the freekeh mixture among the four sheets and top with the fish, capers, tomato, olives, basil, preserved lemon or lemon zest, garlic, pepper and capsicum (if using). Lastly, drizzle with a little olive oil.

Seal the 'bag' by folding in the sides and ends (fasten with a metal paper clip if you need to). Place on a baking tray and bake for 7 minutes (or cook on a hot barbecue).

Serve each closed bag in a shallow bowl.

Balinese Seafood Skewers (DF, GF)

These skewers mean Christmas to me, but any time in summer is a good enough reason to make them. The paste has a few ingredients, so if you're short on time, buy a ready-made one – just make sure it contains nothing but natural ingredients.

SERVES 4

2½ tbsp sunflower oil or rice bran oil
6 green prawns, peeled and deveined
200 g boneless, firm white fish fillets (such as flathead, redfish or wild barramundi), skin off
1 cup grated or flaked coconut
4 long bamboo skewers, soaked in water for 5 minutes, or 3 lemongrass stems
1 short cucumber, cut into large dice
1 red Asian shallot, thinly sliced
½ cup roughly chopped coriander
1 tsp sea salt
1 tbsp lime juice

SPICE PASTE

6 French shallots, peeled and roughly chopped
4 garlic cloves, roughly chopped
3 long red chillies, deseeded and chopped
2 bird's eye chillies, deseeded and chopped
2-cm piece of galangal, peeled and sliced
1 lemongrass stem, white part only, roughly chopped
1 tbsp grated fresh turmeric
1 tbsp coriander leaves and stems, roughly chopped
½ tsp cracked black peppercorns
½ tsp freshly grated nutmeg
1 tbsp lime zest
1 tsp sea salt, or to taste

For the spice paste, in a blender or mortar and pestle, blitz or pound together all the ingredients. You may need to use a little water to bring it together.

Heat ½ tablespoon of the oil in a frying pan over low heat, add the spice paste and gently fry until fragrant, about 1 minute. Cool slightly.

Meanwhile, place the seafood in a processor (or use a stick blender) along with the coconut and fried spice paste and blitz until minced.

Mould about 2 tablespoons of the seafood mixture around the skewers or lemongrass stems. Chill for 30–60 minutes, so the skewers hold together when you're cooking them.

Grill, barbecue or pan-fry the skewers in the remaining oil until golden on all sides.

Make a salad by tossing together the cucumber, shallot, coriander, salt and lime juice in a bowl.

Serve the salad on the side of the skewers.

Seafood Balls with Green Curry Sauce (DF, GF)

Galangal is part of the ginger family, but is not always as easy to find fresh. It has a different flavour to ginger so you can't substitute one for the other. If you can't find it in your supermarket or Asian grocery store, it's okay to leave it out. You can sometimes find it sliced and dried in the latter, though. Soak the dried galangal in water before chopping.

SERVES 4

Curry Paste

1 tsp white peppercorns
½ tsp coriander seeds
1½ tsp cumin seeds
pinch of salt
2 long green chillies, deseeded and chopped
¼ red onion, chopped
4 garlic cloves, chopped
2 lemongrass stems, white part only, chopped
1 tsp peeled and chopped galangal
1 tbsp chopped coriander stems and roots
1 kaffir lime leaf, sliced
1 tsp fish sauce or 1 anchovy fillet

Balls

8 green prawns, peeled and deveined
8 scallops
2 kaffir lime leaves, thinly sliced
1 spring onion, thinly sliced
1 tsp fish sauce
1 handful of Thai basil leaves
1 egg

Curry Sauce

1 tsp safflower oil or rice bran oil
400 g tin coconut milk
2 cups fish stock
2 tsp fish sauce, or to taste
1 tsp grated coconut palm sugar or panela
coriander leaves and thinly sliced red chilli, to garnish

For the curry paste, in a mortar and pestle or spice grinder, grind the peppercorns and seeds together, then add the salt. Put this into a small blender (or keep pounding) and add the other ingredients one at a time. Blitz or pound until you have a smooth paste. (Leftover paste will keep in an airtight container in the fridge for a few weeks, or you can freeze it.) Set aside.

For the balls, place all the ingredients in a food processor and blitz until a paste forms. With wet hands, shape the mixture into walnut-sized balls. Put in the fridge while you make the curry sauce.

For the curry sauce, heat the oil in a large frying pan over medium heat. Stir in 2 tablespoons of the curry paste and cook until it becomes fragrant, about 1 minute. Add the coconut milk, stock, fish sauce and palm sugar or panela and simmer until reduced and thickened a little. Gently place the balls in the pan and cook in the sauce. This should take about 5 minutes. You may need to turn them depending on the depth and width of your pan.

To serve, garnish with the coriander leaves and chilli and serve at the table in the pan.

Thai Fried Rice (DF, GF)

There aren't many veggies in this version of Thai fried rice, so it's probably best to serve it with some Asian greens. However, it's so yummy that you'll want to eat it on its own sometimes. Leave out the prawns and fish sauce for a vegetarian option.

SERVES 4

4 tbsp olive oil
2 eggs, beaten
1 tbsp diced red Asian shallots
1 cup diced firm tofu
500 g green prawns, peeled, deveined and chopped
1 tomato, cut into wedges
1 tbsp tamari, or to taste
4 cups cooked biodynamic brown rice, cold
2 cups bean sprouts
1 cup coriander leaves
2 spring onions, sliced on the diagonal
2 tbsp roughly crushed toasted peanuts
1 tsp sesame oil
1 lime, quartered

White Pepper Paste

½ tsp white peppercorns
4 garlic cloves, chopped
¼ cup coriander stems, roughly chopped

Sauce

6 long red chillies, chopped
6 garlic cloves, peeled
½ cup fish sauce
juice of 3 limes
1 tbsp grated coconut palm sugar

For the white pepper paste, pound the white peppercorns in a mortar and pestle, then add the garlic and coriander and pound again to form a rough paste. Set aside.

For the sauce, blitz together the chilli, garlic, fish sauce, lime juice and palm sugar in a food processor or using a stick blender. Set aside.

In a large wok, heat 2 tablespoons of the oil over medium heat, pour in the eggs and gently stir until just cooked. Remove from the wok.

Pour the remaining oil into the wok, add the shallot and sauté over high heat until translucent. Stir in the white pepper paste and cook until fragrant, about 30 seconds. Add the tofu and prawns and stir. Once the prawns have changed colour, add the tomato, tamari and rice, toss and add the bean sprouts and coriander.

Divide among 4 serving bowls and garnish with the spring onions, peanuts, sesame oil and lime wedges. Serve the sauce in a bowl or jug on the side.

Nurturing Asian Mussels (DF, GF)

Even if you don't like mussels, I'd encourage you to make this dish and eat only the broth. The liquid that the mussels create is so tasty, and is also reputed to strengthen the kidneys, thereby aiding longevity and vitality. Leave the chilli out if you like, and if you'd like a more substantial dish, then stir through some cooked brown rice or quinoa before serving. Clams are also an easy substitute for the mussels.

SERVES 4

2 cups filtered water
1 tsp sambal oelek or 1 bird's eye chilli, chopped
1 garlic clove, crushed
1 tbsp grated fresh ginger
2 French shallots, finely diced
2 kaffir lime leaves, sliced
juice of 1 lime
1 tsp fish sauce
¼ cup sake
500 g mussels, scrubbed and debearded
1 cup coriander leaves

Put all the ingredients apart from the mussels and coriander in a large saucepan. Bring to the boil, then drop to a simmer, and allow the broth to reduce by about half. Add the mussels, shake the pan, and cover with the lid. Allow to simmer for 2–3 minutes, or until the mussels have opened. Discard any that haven't opened. Taste for seasoning and adjust if necessary.

Serve, garnished with the coriander leaves.

Poached Fish with Orange and Sesame Sauce (DF, GF)

You can poach a whole fish and serve the sauce on the side, or use fillets as I have done here. Either way it's going to be lovely. The first time I made this dish I used red emperor fillets and it was truly divine. Ocean trout is wonderful as well. Use whatever is available, in season and sustainable.

SERVES 4

2 x 150 g red emperor fillets,
    cut in half
4 slices of fresh ginger
1 tbsp tamari
1 tbsp sichuan pepper (optional)
2 spring onions, finely chopped
1 tbsp snipped chives
1 orange, quartered

SAUCE
2 tbsp sesame seeds
2 tbsp shiro miso
½ cup orange juice
1 tbsp grated coconut palm sugar
1 tbsp tamari
1 tbsp rice wine vinegar
1 tbsp mirin
1 tbsp grated fresh ginger

Place the fish in a large saucepan and cover with water. Add the ginger, tamari and sichuan pepper (if using). Gently poach the fish for about 5 minutes.

Meanwhile, for the sauce, grind the sesame seeds in a mortar and pestle or a spice grinder. Place in a bowl and mix with the miso, orange juice, palm sugar, tamari, vinegar, mirin and ginger. Taste and adjust as you like.

To serve, place the fish in shallow bowls and pour over the sauce. Scatter on the spring onions and chives.

Serve with extra sauce on the side and garnish with the orange wedges.

Whole Sardines Stuffed with Quinoa and Goji Berries (DF, GF)

What a nutrient-packed dish: sardines, quinoa, goji berries, walnuts, olive oil, lemon, pomegranate and parsley. What else do you need?

SERVES 4 AS A SIDE OR STARTER

1 tbsp goji berries, soaked in
  warm water for 10 minutes
1 tbsp walnuts, chopped
juice and grated zest of 1 lemon
½ cup chopped flat-leaf parsley,
  plus extra to garnish
1 tsp each of allspice and ground
  cinnamon
2 tbsp pomegranate molasses
1 tsp sea salt
2 tbsp olive oil
½–1 cup quinoa, cooked
8 whole sardines, cleaned and
  bones removed
lemon wedges, to serve

Preheat the oven to 180°C.

Drain the goji berries and mix with the walnuts, lemon zest and juice, parsley, allspice, cinnamon, pomegranate molasses, salt, oil and quinoa.

Using a teaspoon, stuff each sardine with about 1 tablespoon of the goji berry mixture. You may need a toothpick to hold the stuffing in place. Arrange snugly in a foil-lined baking tray. Cover with foil and bake for 15 minutes, or until the flesh can be gently pulled apart with a fork.

Sprinkle with the extra parsley and serve with the lemon wedges.

Prawns, Mussels and Clams in a Paper Bag (DF, GF)

I am rather partial to cooking seafood in a bag. You just place all the ingredients in the bag, seal it up and cook for only a few minutes. The results are always good, you're not losing any nutrients in discarded liquid, and there's hardly any cleaning up. (Perfect dinner party food.) You may want to have a sheet of foil outside the paper, but it's not necessary.

SERVES 2

4 green large prawns, peeled and deveined
4 mussels, scrubbed and debearded
6 clams
1 garlic clove, crushed
1 handful of flat-leaf parsley, chopped
2 tbsp finely chopped fennel tops
1 tsp saffron threads
2 spring onions, thinly sliced
1 long red chilli, chopped (optional)
sea salt and cracked white or black pepper, to taste
½ cup dry white wine

Preheat the oven to 180°C or a barbecue to high. Prepare four pieces of baking paper about 30 cm square. Stack two pieces, one on top of the other, for each parcel.

Divide the seafood, garlic, parsley, fennel, saffron, spring onions and chilli in half and place in the centre of each stack of paper. Add seasoning. Transfer the parcels to a baking tray, or a foil tray if using the barbecue, and fold in the edges to create a sort of a bowl. Carefully pour half the wine into each parcel. Fold the top over and seal the 'bags'. Place in the oven for 10 minutes or on the hot barbecue for about 5 minutes. The seafood will continue to cook in the sealed bag.

Serve, sealed in the bag in a shallow bowl.

Honey Soy Salmon with Buckwheat Noodles (DF, GF)

Kudzu is a root related to arrowroot. It is highly prized in Eastern medicine for its positive effect on the digestive system. It is available powdered or as little white 'rocks' from Asian grocery stores or health food stores.

SERVES 2

150 g 100 per cent buckwheat
  noodles
2 x 150 g wild salmon fillets, skin off
1 tsp olive oil
1 tsp kudzu, mixed with ½ cup
  filtered water
2 spring onions, sliced on the
  diagonal, or chives, snipped into
  thirds

MARINADE
½ cup raw honey
2 tbsp tamari
1 tbsp grated fresh ginger
1 tsp mirin
1 cup filtered water

Cook the noodles following the instructions on the packet. Drain, rinse, drain again and set aside.

For the marinade, mix together the honey, tamari, ginger, mirin and water in a shallow bowl.

Add the fish to the marinade, turn to coat, and marinate in the fridge for at least 10 minutes but no longer than 24 hours, flipping the fish a couple of times.

Take the fish out of the marinade and shake off any excess. Pour the marinade into a saucepan and bring to a simmer. Add the fish, cover and poach for 5 minutes, or until the fish is opaque or done to your liking.

Divide the noodles between two shallow bowls. Remove the fish from the pan and place on top of the noodles. Slowly pour the kudzu slurry into the marinade in the pan, whisking to prevent lumps. Simmer for about 1 minute, or until the sauce has thickened.

To serve, pour the sauce over the fish and sprinkle with the spring onions or chives.

VEGETARIAN

I think it's true that most of us don't eat enough vegetables. I believe that the bulk of our diet should come from the plant kingdom, especially veggies in season, which are tastier, cheaper and higher in antioxidants and fibre. Enjoying a meat-free meal and feeling completely satiated is so rewarding. It is possible to eat very well without using any animal products, and once you know how, you won't ever miss them. In this chapter, I have included many vegan meals.

'... IT IS MY VIEW THAT A VEGETARIAN MANNER OF LIVING BY ITS PURELY PHYSICAL EFFECT ON THE HUMAN TEMPERAMENT WOULD MOST BENEFICIALLY INFLUENCE THE LOT OF MANKIND.' ~ ALBERT EINSTEIN

Miso Soup (DF, GF, V, VG)

White radish or daikon has many virtues, including anti-viral properties.
It is usually readily available, although almost any veggie – corn, zucchini,
green beans, Asian greens – will work. If you feel like it, add some buckwheat
or quinoa noodles to the pan before adding the veggies, or serve with cooked
brown rice or quinoa. This is very definitely one of my favourite
and most regularly eaten dishes.

SERVES 4

1 leek, white part only, sliced
1 tbsp olive oil
1 tbsp grated fresh ginger
1 garlic clove, crushed
1 tbsp chopped coriander stems
1 carrot, julienned
½ cup julienned white radish
   (daikon)
1 cup broccoli florets and stems
2 cups filtered water
2 sachets vegan dashi, or 1 litre
   vegetable stock
1 stick of kombu (if available)
4 shiitake mushrooms, sliced
1 tbsp tamari
1 tsp sesame oil
¼ cup miso (shiro or genmai)
200 g silken tofu, sliced into eight
   pieces
2 spring onions, thinly sliced
1 cup coriander leaves
¼ sheet of nori, cut into thin strips
   (optional)

Sauté the leek in the oil in a saucepan over medium heat, then stir in the ginger, garlic and coriander stems and sauté until soft. Add the carrot, white radish and broccoli stems and stir to coat. Add the water, dashi or stock, kombu and mushrooms. Simmer for 7 minutes until the veggies are tender. Turn down the heat and stir in the broccoli florets, tamari and sesame oil. Finally, stir though the miso paste until dissolved, then turn off the heat. Do not boil, as boiling kills the live enzymes in miso.

To serve, ladle the soup into four serving bowls, add the tofu and garnish with the spring onions, coriander leaves and nori (if using).

Crisp Tofu with Kahah Sauce (GF, V)

This sauce, inspired by Afghan cuisine, is rich in spices, and the yoghurt makes it beautifully creamy. The big flavour lends itself perfectly to tofu's neutral taste. Leave the yoghurt out for a vegan alternative.

SERVES 4

2 cups cubed firm tofu
⅓ cup tamari
2 cups plain yoghurt
2 garlic cloves, peeled
1 tbsp ground coriander seeds
½–¾ tsp cayenne pepper or chilli paste
1 tbsp ground cumin
1 tbsp ground turmeric
1 tsp ground ginger
½ onion, diced
2 tbsp roughly chopped coriander leaves and stems
dash of lemon juice or rice vinegar
½ tsp cracked white pepper
2 tbsp safflower oil or rice bran oil
2 spring onions and ½ cup coriander leaves, chopped, to serve

Cover the tofu with the tamari and set aside to marinate while you make the sauce.

Blend the yoghurt, garlic, coriander seeds, cayenne pepper or chilli paste, ground spices, onion, chopped coriander, lemon juice or vinegar and white pepper until smooth. Transfer to a small saucepan and simmer for about 5 minutes, or until it thickens a little.

Drain the tofu and pat dry with paper towel, then fry in the oil in a frying pan over medium–high heat until golden on all sides. Drain on paper towel.

Garnish the tofu with the spring onion and coriander leaves and serve on a platter with the sauce poured over the top.

Veggie and Herb Stack with Buffalo Mozzarella (GF, V)

This is a lovely starter to a late summer or early autumn lunch. Eggplant and zucchini would be nice also. Pan-fry some firm tofu slices and add to the layers for a complete meal. Leave out the mozzarella for a vegan alternative.

SERVES 4

ROAST TOMATO
2 large tomatoes, cut in half
2 tsp olive oil
1 tsp balsamic vinegar
½ tsp sea salt

SWEET POTATO
4 x 1-cm thick rounds of sweet potato
1 tbsp olive oil
½ tsp each of sea salt and cracked
   black pepper
1 large ball of buffalo mozzarella,
   sliced into four
8 basil leaves, to garnish
4 thyme sprigs, to garnish

DRESSING
⅓ cup each of finely chopped flat-leaf
   parsley, mint and basil
½ cup extra virgin olive oil
1 tsp sea salt, to taste
1 tsp capers, rinsed, squeezed dry
   and chopped
1 tsp white wine vinegar

Preheat the oven to 180°C.

For the roast tomato, place the tomatoes on a baking tray and drizzle with the oil, balsamic and salt. Roast for 20 minutes, or until softened.

For the sweet potato, pan-fry the sweet potato with the oil and salt and pepper in a large frying pan over medium heat. Cook on both sides until tender. Set aside.

For the dressing, mix together all the ingredients in a small bowl.

To assemble, place a slice of sweet potato on each serving plate, top with a roast tomato and a slice of bocconcini, pour on about 2 tablespoons of dressing and garnish with the basil and thyme.

Millet Burgers with Miso and Pumpkin Sauce (DF, V, VG)

This sauce is so good, you'll want to use it on other things aside from these very yummy vegan burgers. It is a good idea to start this recipe a day ahead.

SERVES 2

½ cup millet
1½ cups filtered water
½ cup grated Japanese pumpkin
½ onion, brown or white, diced
1 tbsp finely snipped chives
tamari, to taste
1 tbsp brown rice flour, if needed
¼ cup sesame seeds
1 tbsp olive oil or rice bran oil

SAUCE

1 tbsp shiro miso
1 tbsp hulled tahini (stir the tahini
    before using it as the oil separates)
½ cup chopped Japanese pumpkin,
    steamed
1 tbsp sake or mirin (optional)
1 tbsp grated fresh ginger
sea salt, to taste

TO SERVE

4 spelt sourdough buns
4 iceberg lettuce leaves

To cook the millet, place it in a saucepan and wash well. Drain and add the water. Bring to the boil, then drop to a simmer. Put the lid half on the pan and gently cook over a medium heat until the water has almost evaporated. Taste the millet – it should be just tender. If not, add a little more water. Cover completely with the lid and remove from heat. Let sit, covered, for 10–15 minutes to allow the millet to continue cooking in the steam.

Allow the millet to cool a little, then add to a bowl with the pumpkin, onion, chives and tamari. Mix well. You may need to add the brown rice flour if the mixture is too wet. Cover with a plate or lid and leave in the fridge overnight to firm up. (If you don't have time for this step, you will need to mix in a couple of eggs.)

Shape the millet mixture into patties (the number and size depends on the size of your buns), then roll in the sesame seeds.

To make the sauce, mash the miso, tahini, pumpkin, sake or mirin and ginger, or purée them using a hand-held blender. Taste for seasoning.

Heat the oil in a hot cast-iron or non-stick pan then cook the patties for about 1 minute on each side, until golden.

To serve, spread the inside of each bun with about 1 tablespoon of the sauce, then top with a patty. Finish with a lettuce leaf and close up.

Roasted Japanese Sweet Potato with Cashews (DF, GF, V, VG)

Umeboshi means 'pickled plum' and the vinegar I have used here is made from these plums. It is highly alkaline and quite salty. I use it often as it is not only really good for me but adds a special lift to almost any dish. You should be able to get it from any Asian food store and most health food shops. If you have no luck, then use red wine vinegar or apple cider vinegar instead. Vegans will want to use rice syrup instead of honey.

SERVES 2 AS A SIDE

1 large sweet potato, cut into
    3-cm chunks
1 tbsp rice bran oil
1½ tbsp umeboshi vinegar
1 tsp mirin
1 tbsp light soy sauce
1 tbsp vegan dashi
1 tbsp rice syrup or raw honey
1 cup cashew nuts, toasted
1 small handful coriander leaves or
    sliced spring onions, to garnish

Preheat the oven to 180°C.

Coat the sweet potato in the oil, place on a baking tray and roast for 20–30 minutes, or until golden.

Combine the vinegar, mirin, soy sauce, dashi and rice syrup or honey in a bowl.

While the sweet potato is still warm, pour the dressing over the top.

Serve garnished with the cashews and coriander or spring onions.

Tofu Skewers with Spicy Asian Dressing (DF, GF, V, VG)

You can add veggies to these skewers for a bit of colour and to vary the taste. Thread cubes of capsicum, zucchini, some mushrooms or eggplant in between the tofu before marinating. It is best to start this recipe a day ahead.

MAKES 6 SKEWERS

24 tofu cubes, about 3 cm square
1 tbsp chilli paste or chilli sauce
2 tbsp lime juice
1 tbsp grated coconut palm sugar
2 tbsp vegetable stock

GARNISH
1 tbsp toasted sesame seeds
6 flat-leaf parsley sprigs

Place the tofu in a bowl and add all the other ingredients. Allow to marinate for at least 30 minutes, but overnight would be better.

Soak 6 wooden skewers in water for 20 minutes so they won't burn on the barbecue (or use metal ones), then thread on the tofu.

Cook on a hot barbecue or under a grill for 1 minute on each side, or until the tofu starts to turn golden brown. Garnish with the sesame seeds and parsley and serve on a big platter.

Mushroom and Kale Frittata
(DF, GF, V)

I love having a frittata in the fridge. It's great for breakfast or lunch with a salad or as a grain-free dinner. Try it with some Green Tahini Dressing (*see* page 104), wrapped in flatbread and toasted. Or halve the recipe, then transfer all ingredients into a six-hole muffin tray. Cook for 15–20 minutes at 180°C.

SERVES 4–6

1 leek, white part only, sliced
1–2 tbsp olive oil
1 tsp sea salt
3 cups halved mushrooms (Swiss, shiitake and/or button mushrooms)
2 garlic cloves, crushed
2 cups kale or silverbeet, roughly chopped
6 eggs
1 cup basil leaves, torn
½ cup soy milk
2 tsp dijon or wholegrain mustard
½ tsp each of sea salt and cracked black pepper, or to taste
1 tomato, thinly sliced

Slowly sauté the leek with the olive oil and salt in a large ovenproof frying pan (cast iron is great) over low heat. This should take about 10 minutes. The leek will become very sweet and soft. Increase the heat to medium and add the mushrooms. Sauté for 2 minutes, or until soft. Toss in the garlic and cook for 2 minutes. Drop the heat to low and toss in the kale or silverbeet and stir. Cover with the lid and remove from the heat.

Preheat the oven to 100°C.

Whisk together the eggs, basil, soy milk, mustard and seasoning and gently pour into the pan. Place the pan over low heat for a minute or so, so the bottom of the frittata cooks slightly and forms a crust. Overlap the tomato slices on top, then place in the oven for about 40 minutes, or until the egg is set and just starting to turn a golden colour.

Let the frittata cool before slicing into wedges or thin slices.

Millet Patties
(DF, GF, V, VG)

This is one of those recipes that begs to be made up and frozen, ready for you to thaw on those days when cooking isn't – or can't be – on your agenda. Add a quick salad and some tamari seeds (I usually have these in my pantry) and life is good.

SERVES 4

1 cup millet grain
2½ cups filtered water
½ brown onion, diced
1½ tbsp coconut oil
1 garlic clove, chopped
1 carrot, grated
1 zucchini, grated and squeezed dry
2 tsp ground or grated fresh turmeric
2 tsp garam masala
1 tsp tamari, or to taste

Place the millet in a saucepan and wash well. Drain and add the water. Bring to the boil, then drop to a simmer. Put the lid half on the pan and gently cook over a medium heat until the water has almost evaporated. Taste the millet – it should be just tender. If not, add a little more water. Cover completely with the lid and remove from heat. Sit, covered, for 10–15 minutes to allow the millet to continue cooking in the steam.

Meanwhile, in a large frying pan over medium heat, sauté the onion in 1 tablespoon of the oil until translucent. Add the garlic and veggies and keep cooking for another minute. Stir in the spices (you may need to add a few drops of water to prevent them from sticking), and cook until the veggies have softened. Transfer to a bowl and allow the mixture to cool. Then add the cooked millet and the tamari and stir to combine. Set aside. Leaving the mixture in the fridge overnight will help to hold the patties together.

Using your hands, roll the millet mixture into balls about 5 cm in diameter, squeeze firmly then flatten into patties (it should make about eight to ten). In a large frying pan, heat the remaining oil over medium heat and fry the patties until golden brown on both sides. (Alternatively, you can bake the patties for 15 minutes in a 180°C oven. Brush with a little oil first.)

Drain on paper towel.

Spinach and Ricotta Tart (V)

You could fill this easy tart base with anything you like, sweet or savoury.
For a gluten-free version, use ground almonds instead of the spelt flour and dust
with brown rice flour; this dough, however, won't hold together as well,
as gluten helps to bind the ingredients.

SERVES 4

PASTRY

3 cups spelt flour, plus extra
   for dusting
1 tsp ground cinnamon
½ tsp sea salt
½ cup safflower oil
½ cup chilled filtered water

FILLING

250 g fresh ricotta cheese
2 eggs
pinch of ground cinnamon
3 cups roughly chopped baby spinach
1 tsp sea salt

Preheat the oven to 180°C. Lightly brush a 20-cm round tart tin with a removable base with a little oil.

For the pastry, in a large bowl, combine the dry ingredients, then add the oil. Using a knife, bring the mixture together, slowly adding the water to form a fairly dry and short dough. Knead on a lightly floured surface for 5 minutes. Shape into a ball, then cover with plastic wrap and chill for 30 minutes.

Dust the pastry with a little spelt flour and roll out to about 3 mm thick. Place the pastry in the prepared tin. Line the pastry shell with a piece of baking paper and pour in some baking beads, uncooked rice or dried legumes. Blind bake for 10 minutes. Remove the paper and beads and allow to cool.

For the filling, mix together the ricotta, eggs, cinnamon, spinach and salt in a bowl.

Fill the pastry shell with the filling and bake for 10 minutes, or until it has turned slightly golden. Cool slightly, then serve.

Mediterranean Stuffed Veggies
(DF, GF, V, VG)

Add some mashed firm tofu or legumes to this dish to add more protein,
or serve these veggies as a side with some marinated tofu or fish.

SERVES 4

½ cup millet
1½ cups filtered water
1 garlic clove, finely grated
2 tbsp olive oil
1 eggplant, halved, flesh partly
    scooped out and chopped
2 large zucchini, halved, flesh partly
    scooped out and chopped
½ cup mixed herbs (such as oregano,
    flat-leaf parsley, thyme and/or
    basil), chopped
¼ cup pitted olives, any type,
    roughly chopped
1 tbsp capers, rinsed and squeezed
    dry
zest of 1 lemon
1 red capsicum, halved and deseeded
2 large tomatoes, halved and deseeded

Preheat the oven to 180°C.

Place the millet in a saucepan and wash well. Drain and add the water. Bring to the boil, then drop to a simmer. Put the lid half on and gently cook over a medium heat until the water has almost evaporated. Taste the millet – it should be just tender. If not, add a little more water. Completely cover with the lid and remove from heat. Let sit, covered, for 10–15 minutes to allow the millet to continue cooking in the steam.

In a large frying pan, lightly sauté the garlic in 1 tablespoon of the oil for about 10 seconds over low to medium heat. Stir in the chopped flesh from the eggplant and zucchini and cook for 5 minutes, or until the veggies have softened a little. Allow the mixture to cool, then add the millet, herbs, olives, capers and lemon zest. Stuff this mixture into the capsicum and tomato halves, place on a baking tray and drizzle with the remaining oil. Bake for about 20 minutes, or until the veggies are soft.

Falafel with Carrot Salad and Green Tahini Dressing (DF, V, VG)

I grew up on falafel, hummus and tabouleh, so this trio is like coming home to me.
I have changed things slightly by adding the carrot salad, which is more Israeli
than Lebanese, and made the tahini dressing green by adding coriander. Start this recipe
the day before. Leave out the bread for a gluten-free version.

SERVES 2

Falafel
1 cup dried chickpeas, soaked in
    water overnight, then drained
1 onion, chopped
1 tsp ground cumin
½ cup chopped coriander leaves
    and stems
½ cup chopped mint leaves
1 garlic clove, crushed
2 tbsp brown rice flour
1 tsp sea salt
2 tbsp rice bran oil or olive oil plus
    extra for frying

Salad
2 cups grated carrot
½ cup raisins
½ cup orange juice

Green Tahini Dressing
⅓ cup hulled tahini (stir the tahini
    before using it as the oil separates)
½ cup coriander leaves
½ tsp ground cumin
½ tsp cayenne pepper (optional)
juice of 2 lemons
1 garlic clove, crushed
1 tsp sea salt

To Serve
wholemeal pitta bread

For the falafel, combine all the ingredients except the oil in a food processor and blitz until a thick paste forms. Keep it a little chunky. Place the mixture in the fridge while you prepare the sides.

For the salad, mix together the carrot, raisins and orange juice in a bowl. Set aside.

For the tahini, process all the ingredients in a food processor, or mix together in a bowl with a fork. Taste and adjust the seasoning and/or consistency using a little more water or lemon juice, if needed.

Using about 1 tablespoon for each falafel, mould the falafel mixture into football shapes with your hands. Heat the oil in a frying pan over high heat and shallow- or deep-fry the falafel in batches until golden on all sides, without overcrowding your pan. (It's up to you how much oil you use to fry them.) Drain on paper towel.

Serve the falafel on a platter with the pitta bread, salad and tahini.

Mini Corn Fritters (DF, GF, V, VG)

These are perfect for school lunches, not to mention adult lunches. They are an easy finger food, can be eaten in a few minutes and are full of essential nutrients. I've used navy beans in this recipe instead of eggs to bind the ingredients together. Try using other veggies also.

MAKES ABOUT 12

3 tbsp olive oil or rice bran oil
1 small white onion, diced
1 tbsp finely chopped coriander stems
1 garlic clove, crushed
1 cup corn kernels, cut off the cob
1 cup grated sweet potato
1 zucchini, grated and squeezed dry
1 cup cooked navy beans, rinsed
   and drained
½ cup finely chopped mint leaves
½ tbsp sea salt, or to taste
2 tbsp brown rice flour or besan
1 lime, quartered

In a saucepan, heat 1 tablespoon of the oil and sauté the onion and coriander over medium heat until the onion is translucent. Now add the garlic and stir for a few seconds. Next add the veggies, stir to coat in the oil and sauté for 1 minute until the veggies start to cook. Remove from the heat.

Place the navy beans in a bowl and mash with a fork. Add the veggie mixture, mint and salt. Slowly mix in the flour until you have a firm mixture that you can roll into balls. Taste for seasoning. Shape into 12 balls about the size of a walnut, then press into patties.

Heat the remaining oil in a large frying pan and fry the fritters, in batches of six to eight, depending on the size of your pan, until golden on each side. Drain on paper towel.

Serve the fritters with the lime quarters.

Mediterranean Baked Beans with Feta (GF, V)

Making your own baked beans takes so little time that there really isn't a good excuse to buy the salty, refined, sugary ones in a tin. Leave out the oregano, feta and rocket if you're after straight-up baked beans or just the feta for a vegan alternative, but leaving them in makes them Mediterranean.

SERVES 4

1 tbsp olive oil
1 red onion, sliced
2 garlic cloves, crushed (optional)
2 x 400 g tins navy or butter beans, rinsed and drained
700 g tomato passata (or 2 x 400 g tins crushed tomatoes)
1 tbsp tomato paste
1 tbsp dijon mustard
1–2 tbsp grated coconut palm sugar or panela
1 tbsp fresh oregano leaves or 1 tsp dried oregano
2 tsp sea salt, or to taste
1 cup crumbled goat's feta
1 large handful of rocket
cracked black pepper

In a saucepan over medium heat, heat the oil and sauté the onion until translucent. Add the garlic (if using) and stir for a few seconds. Now add the beans, passata or crushed tomatoes and tomato paste, mustard, sugar, oregano and salt. Stir and simmer for about 5 minutes, or until the sugar has dissolved. Crumble the feta over the top, then put under a hot grill for a few minutes until a golden crust forms.

To serve, pile the rocket on top and finish with some pepper.

Polenta with Lentils and Mushrooms (DF, GF, V, VG)

Polenta is ground corn, which is why it is sometimes referred to as cornmeal. It is available finely or coarsely ground. Once considered peasant food by the Italians – as it was cheap, bland and filling – these days we prize it for its nutritional value, lack of gluten and versatility.

SERVES 4

8 dried porcini or shiitake
  mushrooms
3 cups vegetable stock
1 cup fine polenta

LENTILS
1 tbsp olive oil
½ brown onion, diced
2 celery stalks, diced
1 carrot, chopped
1–2 garlic cloves, crushed
2 cups vegetable stock
1 bay leaf
1 cup puy lentils or tiny blue-green
  lentils, washed
1 tbsp fresh thyme leaves or 1 tsp
  dried thyme
sea salt and cracked black pepper,
  to taste
½ cup finely chopped basil or flat-
  leaf parsley, or 1–2 bay leaves, to
  garnish

Place the mushrooms in a small bowl, add enough warm water to cover and soak for a few minutes until soft. Drain, reserving the liquid, then slice and set aside.

For the lentils, heat the oil in a large saucepan over medium heat, and sauté the onion, celery, carrot and garlic for 5 minutes until starting to soften. Add the stock, bay leaf, sliced mushrooms, lentils and thyme and bring to the boil. Drop to a simmer and cook for 30 minutes, or until the lentils are tender. Taste for seasoning – you may not need any salt and pepper depending on what stock you use. Cook for 30 minutes with the lid half on.

Meanwhile, bring the stock to a rolling simmer in a large saucepan over high heat and add the liquid reserved from soaking the mushrooms. Rain in the polenta and whisk for about 1 minute, or until all the liquid has been absorbed. Cook over low heat, stirring frequently, for another few minutes until the polenta has softened and become creamy.

To serve, spoon the wet polenta into a shallow bowl, make an indentation in the centre using the back of your spoon, and ladle in the lentils. Garnish with the extra bay leaves or the basil or parsley.

Chickpea and Harissa Tagine with Quinoa (GF, V)

Harissa is a spice paste, originating in North Africa. It is delicious in curries, or try it as an alternative to tomato sauce, stirred through soup just before serving, as a coating for fish or tofu before grilling, or you could make harissa hummus. You may want to double or even triple this harissa recipe as it will keep in the fridge in an airtight container for as long as you keep the top covered with a thin layer of olive oil. Try adding 1 teaspoon of ground fennel seeds, 3 tablespoons of red wine vinegar and the same amount of lemon juice for harissa with a twist. If you can find them, dried chilli peppers are traditionally used instead of capsicum. To make a dairy-free and vegan option, leave out the dollop of yoghurt or use coconut milk yoghurt or the Green Tahini Dressing (*see* page 104).

SERVES 4

½ cup each of red and white quinoa
  or 1 cup tri-coloured quinoa
4 cups filtered water

HARISSA
2 red capsicums
4 garlic cloves, unpeeled
2 tbsp olive oil
1 tsp coriander seeds
1 tsp caraway seeds
1 tsp cayenne pepper
1 tsp sea salt

TAGINE
1 onion, brown or white, sliced
1 tbsp olive oil
2 garlic cloves, crushed
½ tbsp grated fresh ginger
1 tbsp each of flat-leaf parsley and
  coriander stems, finely chopped
1 tsp ground cumin
1 tsp sweet or smoked paprika
400 g tin chickpeas, rinsed and
  drained
2 cups unpeeled chopped Japanese
  pumpkin
400 g tin chopped tomatoes
  or 2 cups vegetable stock
1 tbsp thinly sliced preserved lemon
1 tsp saffron threads (optional)
sea salt

TO SERVE
1 small handful each flat-leaf parsley
  and coriander leaves, chopped
4 lemon wedges
plain yoghurt (optional)

Combine the quinoa and water in a saucepan and bring to the boil. Drop to a simmer, put the lid half on and let cook until the water has been absorbed and little 'volcano holes' appear in the quinoa. This will take 10–15 minutes. Taste at this point; the quinoa should be tender and almost cooked. If not, add a splash more water. Put the lid on and turn the heat off. Allow the quinoa to steam for another 10 minutes, or until you're ready to serve.

For the harissa, place the capsicums, garlic and oil in a frying pan over medium to high heat. Cook until the capsicum and garlic skins start to turn black all over. Place the capsicums and garlic in a plastic bag and let sweat for a few minutes. Remove from the bag and remove the skin from the capsicums and garlic. Place the capsicums and garlic in a food processor and blitz with the spices until a smooth paste forms. Season.

For the tagine, slowly cook the onion in the oil in a frying pan over medium heat until the onion is translucent. Stir in the garlic, ginger and chopped parsley and coriander stems. Add the spices and cook until fragrant and starting to stick to the base of the pan. Stir in the chickpeas and pumpkin, then add 1 tablespoon of the harissa and stir so that everything is coated with the harissa. Add the tomatoes or stock, preserved lemon and saffron (if using) and simmer at least until the pumpkin is tender, but the longer the better. Taste for seasoning; you may want to add some salt.

Garnish with the parsley and coriander leaves and lemon wedges and serve with the quinoa in a separate dish on the side. You may want a little yoghurt or harissa on the side also.

Adzuki and Pumpkin Rissoles (GF, V)

This is my version of a traditional macrobiotic recipe. It is best known as a casserole, but I've turned it into patties. The seaweed commonly used is kombu, but it is proving more and more difficult to find in Australia, so I've replaced it with arame. This is a perfectly balanced, highly nutritious, yummy, vegan alternative to a meat rissole. Leave out the yoghurt for a dairy-free and vegan option or use hummus. You could also try it with Green Tahini Dressing (*see* page 104).

MAKES 12

400 g tin adzuki beans, rinsed
  and drained
1 onion, brown or white, diced
½ tbsp grated fresh ginger
1 garlic clove, crushed
2 cups chopped Japanese pumpkin
  or sweet potato, steamed
pinch of arame, soaked in water until
  soft, then drained
2 tbsp finely snipped chives
½ cup finely chopped coriander
1 tsp tamari, or to taste
½ tsp sesame oil
½ cup brown rice flour, plus extra
  for dusting
1 tbsp olive oil, for frying
plain yoghurt, to serve (optional)

Put the beans in a large bowl and mash with a fork. Add the other ingredients (except the yoghurt) and mix well. Shape into 12 patties and dust with the extra flour. Cook on the barbecue or in batches in a large frying pan over medium to high heat for about 1 minute on each side, or until golden.

Serve with yoghurt.

Spaghetti with Smoked Tofu and Kale (DF, V, VG)

Smoked tofu is a really good product to have in your fridge. The smoky flavour it imparts creates a whole new dimension. Missing bacon? Try smoked tofu. Use gluten-free pasta if you're avoiding gluten.

SERVES 4

400 g spelt spaghetti
4 finely shredded cups kale
1 tbsp olive oil
1½ cups diced smoked tofu
2 garlic cloves
1 cup diced tomatoes
1 tsp dried chilli flakes (optional)
3 tbsp vegan pesto
grated zest and juice of 1 lemon

Cook the pasta in boiling salted water according to the packet directions. Place the kale in a colander and drain the pasta over the top. This will wilt the kale. Run some cool water over the pasta and kale and drain well.

Heat the oil in a large frying pan, add the tofu, stir to coat, and cook for 1 minute, until it starts to become golden. Add the garlic, tomatoes and chilli flakes (if using) and simmer for about 30 seconds, until the tomatoes have just started to soften. Stir through the pesto and taste for seasoning.

Add the pasta and kale to the pan and gently toss. Finish with the lemon zest and juice.

Tofu with Cashews and Chilli Jam (DF, GF, V, VG)

This has all the flavours of Thailand without the white sugar and salty soy sauce. Serve this with brown rice if you like.

SERVES 4

1 cup cashew nuts
2 tbsp safflower oil or rice bran oil
3 cups diced firm tofu
1 tbsp olive oil
2 garlic cloves, finely chopped
1 tbsp thinly sliced ginger
2 bunches of broccolini, trimmed
   and halved
1 red capsicum, sliced
2 large handfuls of snow peas,
   strings off
1 tsp tamari
½ tsp sesame oil

CHILLI JAM
2 long red chillies, chopped
2 dried long red chillies or
   1–2 tsp dried chilli flakes
1 tbsp tomato paste
½ tbsp rice wine vinegar
1 French shallot, finely diced

To make the chilli jam, blitz all the ingredients in a food processor to form a paste. Set aside.

Toast the cashews in a dry wok until golden brown, then set aside. Add the safflower or rice bran oil to the hot wok and fry the tofu until golden and crisp. Drain on paper towel.

Heat the olive oil in the wok and fry the garlic and ginger for a few seconds until fragrant, then add the vegetables and stir-fry for about 1 minute (the veggies need to be a little crunchy). Return the tofu and cashews to the wok, then stir in the chilli jam. Finish with a splash of tamari and the sesame oil.

Okra with Cashews
(DF, GF, V, VG)

We don't use a lot of okra in Australia, which is a shame, considering how easy it is to prepare, its nutritional and medicinal value, and the thickening effect it creates in soups and stews. And it's economical to use. Add some lemon juice or vinegar to help reduce the gooey texture.

SERVES 4 AS A SIDE

1 tbsp olive oil
2 cups trimmed and roughly
   chopped okra
1 tomato, diced
2 spring onions, sliced on the
   diagonal
zest of 1 lemon (or use 1 tbsp fresh
   lemon thyme instead)
1 tbsp fresh thyme leaves or 1 tsp
   dried thyme
1 tbsp shiro miso, dissolved in
   ¼ cup warm water
1 tsp each sea salt and cracked black
   pepper, or to taste
1 cup cashew nuts, toasted

Heat a frying pan over medium heat, pour in the oil, toss in the okra and cook for 2 minutes. Add the tomato, spring onions, lemon zest (or lemon thyme), thyme and miso and cook over medium heat for about 5 minutes. Taste for seasoning. Stir the cashews through just before serving.

Silverbeet and Chickpeas with Tahini Sauce (DF, GF, V, VG)

My Lebanese grandma used to make this for herself all the time in her
later years. As a girl I thought everyone ate this. I have added the ground cumin
and tahini sauce, although both are used in Middle Eastern cooking.
Sometimes I use kale instead of silverbeet.

SERVES 4

1 tbsp olive oil
1 onion, sliced
1 tsp ground cumin
1 garlic clove, finely chopped
4 large handfuls silverbeet, washed
   and roughly chopped
1 tsp sea salt
400 g tin chickpeas, rinsed and
   drained

TAHINI SAUCE
½ cup hulled tahini (stir the tahini
   before using it as the oil separates)
juice of ½–1 lemon
1 garlic clove, finely grated
pinch of sea salt
water, to thin out

Heat a frying pan over medium heat. Add the oil and
onion and sauté until the onion is soft and starting to
turn golden. Stir in the cumin and garlic and continue
to cook for another minute. Add the silverbeet and salt
and, using tongs, toss with the onion. Cover with the lid
and cook for about 3 minutes, or until the silverbeet has
wilted. Add the chickpeas, turn the heat off and mash
with a fork so the chickpeas break down a little.

To make the tahini sauce, combine the tahini, lemon
juice, garlic and salt in a bowl and whisk. It will look as
though the sauce has curdled but keep whisking, adding
a little water or lemon juice if the sauce is too thick. Keep
whisking and adding water or lemon juice, to taste, until
smooth and creamy.

To serve, pile the silverbeet and chickpeas on a platter
and generously pour the tahini sauce over the top.

Corn on the Cob with Mexican Molcajete Sauce (DF, GF, V, VG)

It's really worth chargrilling your tomatoes and chillies before you peel
and blitz them. It takes their flavour to a whole other place. This smoky sauce
goes beautifully with the corn, but you'll find so many other reasons to make it.

SERVES 4

2 ripe tomatoes
6 long red chillies
2 bird's eye chillies
1 tsp olive oil, for the barbecue
2 garlic cloves
1 tsp cumin seeds, toasted
1 tsp smoked paprika
juice of ½ lime
1 tsp sea salt
4 corn cobs, husks and silk removed

To Serve
¼ red onion, thinly sliced
1 small handful coriander leaves
1 lime, cut into quarters

Place the chillies and tomatoes on a hot, oiled barbecue
and roast until soft and chargrilled. Cool slightly, then
remove the skins.

Now place the chillies, garlic, cumin seeds and paprika
in a blender and blitz (or pound in a mortar and pestle)
until a rough paste forms. Add the tomatoes and
continue processing/pounding until the sauce looks
quite smooth. Finish with the lime juice and salt.

Barbecue, roast or steam the corn until tender.

Place the corn on a platter and pour the sauce over the
top. Garnish with the onion, coriander leaves and lime
cheeks.

Veggie and Tofu Gado Gado Pies (DF, V, VG)

This peanut sauce is intense and wonderful. I've made this recipe into small pies because you only need a small amount, but feel free to thin the sauce out a little with water and make one big pie.

MAKES 6 SMALL PIES

PASTRY
1½ cups white spelt flour
1½ cups wholemeal spelt flour
pinch of sea salt
½ cup safflower oil or rice bran oil
½ cup iced water

PEANUT SAUCE
½ onion, diced
1 tbsp olive oil
2 garlic cloves, crushed
1 tbsp grated fresh ginger
1 lemongrass stem, white part only, bruised
1 tsp ground cumin
1 tsp ground turmeric
1 tsp paprika
1 tsp chilli powder
3–4 cups filtered water
½ cup organic crunchy peanut butter
1 kaffir lime leaf, thinly sliced
1 tbsp tamarind purée
1 tbsp tamari, or to taste

FILLING
1 large handful of green beans, cut into 2-cm pieces
1 small carrot, diced
1 cup diced firm tofu

For the pastry, combine the flours and salt in a bowl, then slowly drizzle in the oil and, using a fork, mix until the consistency of breadcrumbs. Now drizzle in the water and continue to stir with the fork until the pastry comes together to form a ball. Knead on a lightly floured surface for 5 minutes, and until the pastry is smooth and pliable. Shape into a ball, cover with plastic wrap and chill for 30 minutes.

For the peanut sauce, sauté the onion in the oil in a frying pan over medium heat until soft. Stir in the garlic, ginger and lemongrass and cook for another minute. Now add the spices and cook for 1 minute, stirring frequently. Stir in 2 cups of water, the peanut butter, kaffir lime leaf and tamarind. Simmer gently for about 10 minutes, stirring frequently. Add more water, about 1–2 cups, as the sauce thickens. Stir in the tamari and set aside.

Preheat the oven to 180°C. Lightly grease a six-hole muffin tin.

Meanwhile, roll out the pastry between two sheets of baking paper until about 3 mm thick. Use a 150-mm round pastry cutter to cut out six rounds for the base and press into the prepared tin. Cut out six pastry lids with a slightly smaller round cutter.

For the filling, lightly steam the beans and carrot, place in a bowl, then gently mix in the tofu. Pour on the peanut sauce and stir to combine.

Spoon the filling into each pastry case and seal with a pastry lid. Cut a small slit in each lid. Bake for about 20 minutes, or until the pastry is golden brown.

PARTY FOOD

Hors d'oeuvres and finger food needn't contain highly processed ingredients to taste good. They can and should be little bundles of joy in your mouth that heal and nurture you, as well as taste delicious. They are just a bite or two, something to stimulate your appetite to get you ready for the main meal, or something to have with drinks. Some of the recipes in here can double as an entrée for a dinner party or as a meal on their own.

INDIAN CAULIFLOWER FRITTERS

CHARGRILLED SPICY CALAMARI

ANTIPASTI VEGGIES

BALINESE GRILLED FISH PEPES

MUNG BEAN FRITTERS

SMOKED TROUT AND FETA MOUSSE WITH CORN BRUSCHETTA

NORI ROLLS WITH TEMPEH, MILLET AND AVOCADO

ZUCCHINI, MINT AND FETA FRITTERS

SAN CHOI BAO

CRAB AND CORN CAKES

EGGPLANT AND ZUCCHINI ROLLS WITH SUNFLOWER
    SEED PESTO AND BOCCONCINI

BETEL LEAVES WITH PRAWNS AND COCONUT

SCALLOPS IN THE SHELL WITH MANGO SALSA

MILLET AND TOFU CROQUETTES

HORS D'OEUVRES 1. (NOUN) APPETIZER, APPETISER, STARTER FOOD OR DRINK TO STIMULATE THE APPETITE (USUALLY SERVED BEFORE A MEAL OR AS THE FIRST COURSE)

Indian Cauliflower Fritters (GF, V)

Deep-frying requires an oil that has a high smoking point. Once an oil 'smokes' then it becomes a carcinogen. So choose rice bran, safflower, organic peanut or sunflower oil. Leave the dressing out if seeking a vegan or dairy-free alternative.

MAKES ABOUT 16

4 cups cauliflower florets, cut into small pieces
1 cup filtered water
1 small onion, diced
1 tbsp coriander stems, finely chopped
2 tbsp olive oil or rice bran oil
1 tbsp grated ginger
2 garlic cloves, crushed
2 tsp each of ground cumin, turmeric and garam masala
2 cups flour (brown rice, fine polenta or besan)
½ tbsp sea salt, or to taste
2 zucchini, grated and squeezed dry
4 eggs
1 cup coriander leaves, plus extra to garnish
2 cups rice bran oil, for deep-frying

YOGHURT DRESSING

½ cup plain yoghurt
1 tbsp olive oil (optional)
zest and juice of 1 lemon
1 tsp ground cumin
1 tbsp roughly chopped coriander leaves
sea salt, to taste, or 1 tsp umeboshi vinegar
1 lime, quartered

Put the cauliflower and water in a large saucepan and simmer (or steam) until the cauliflower becomes very soft; this will take about 20 minutes. Drain in a colander and using the back of a spoon, push out any excess water. Set aside to drain until you're ready to use it.

In a large frying pan over medium heat, sauté the onion and coriander stems in the olive or rice bran oil until the onion is translucent. Add the ginger and garlic and stir for a few seconds. Stir in the spices and cook until they become fragrant and start to stick to the base of the pan. Remove from the heat and set aside.

Combine the flour, salt, zucchini and cauliflower in a bowl and stir well. Add the onion and spice mixture and stir again. Finish off by adding the eggs and coriander leaves. Give the mixture a good mix and leave in the fridge for 30 minutes or so if you can. (Not essential.)

Heat the rice bran oil in a large heavy-based saucepan over medium heat. Test the oil by dropping in a tiny bit of the mixture – it should start to gently fry. Don't have the oil too hot – it shouldn't smoke.

Using two dessertspoons, drop 1 tablespoon of the cauliflower mixture per fritter into the hot oil. Cook in batches. Let them turn golden brown, then flip. Remove the fritters with a slotted spoon and drain them on paper towel.

For the yoghurt dressing, place all the ingredients in a bowl and stir. Taste for seasoning.

Garnish the fritters with extra coriander leaves and the lime wedges and serve with the yoghurt dressing on the side.

Chargrilled Spicy Calamari
(DF, GF)

Cleaning calamari is a bit of a messy job. It's not hard, just messy.
So have your fishmonger do it for you if you prefer, or you can buy cleaned,
frozen tubes. This is a simple and stunning dish.

SERVES 8

4 cleaned calamari tubes
2 tsp sea salt
2 tbsp olive oil
4 long red chillies, thinly sliced
1 cup flat-leaf parsley leaves, roughly
    chopped, plus extra to serve
2–4 garlic cloves
1 tbsp grated lemon zest
cracked black pepper
lemon juice
2 lemons, quartered

Place a knife or spatula inside the calamari to hold it in place. With another knife, slice the calamari across its width at approximately 2-cm intervals. Continue with the rest of the calamari. Now toss it in a little salt.

Heat the olive oil in a large frying pan or on the barbecue and fry the calamari for about 2 minutes on each side. As the calamari is cooking, add the chilli, parsley, garlic, lemon zest and salt and pepper.

To serve, slice the calamari into bite-sized pieces, squeeze on some lemon juice and garnish with the lemon wedges and extra parsley. Have some toothpicks on the serving platter.

Antipasti Veggies (GF, V, VG)

I've always loved how the Italians do this dish. A little bit of this yummy thing, a little bit of that yummy thing. An antipasti platter is enough for a meal. Have the platter ready on your table as guests arrive. Serve with spelt crackers and/or gluten-free crackers. You could leave the marinade out and simpy rub the veggies with olive oil, salt and pepper. Leave the feta out for a dairy-free platter.

SERVES 8

MOROCCAN MARINADE
1½ cups tomato passata
½ cup orange juice
½ cup lemon juice
½ cup tamari
4 garlic cloves
¼ cup raw honey (rice syrup for vegans)
½ tsp dried chilli flakes
1 tsp ground coriander
1 tsp ground fennel
½ tsp ground cinnamon
2 tsp ground cumin
2 tsp grated fresh ginger
1 tbsp balsamic vinegar

VEGGIES
8 portobello mushrooms
4 zucchini, cut in half lengthways
16 asparagus spears
2 small eggplants, cut into 1-cm thick
  slices
200 g tempeh, cut into 1-cm fingers
1 tbsp olive oil
400 g tin low-sodium chickpeas, rinsed
  and drained
1 tbsp preserved lemon, thinly sliced
1 tbsp roughly chopped thyme
1 cup roughly cubed marinated
  goat's feta (leave out if you're vegan)
½ cup roughly chopped basil
Beetroot and Almond Dip
  (*see* page 151)
1 cup olives (your choice of kalamata,
  green, mixed, marinated)

For the Moroccan marinade, place all the ingredients in a blender and process until smooth. This will make about 2 cups. Store what you don't use in an airtight container in the fridge for a week or freeze for up to 3 months.

For the veggies, place all the veggies and tempeh on a large platter and cover with the marinade. Turn so that both sides are covered. Leave to marinate for as long as you have time (from 5 minutes to overnight).

Before cooking the veggies and tempeh, scrape off any excess marinade. Cook the veggies and tempeh, in batches, in a hot, oiled chargrill pan until each is chargrilled to your liking. Turn often and brush regularly with more marinade.

Combine the chickpeas, preserved lemon and thyme in a bowl and set aside.

To assemble, place the veggies and tempeh on a large platter and add the beetroot and almond dip, chickpeas, feta and olives.

Balinese Grilled Fish Pepes
(DF, GF)

Pepes are pieces of fish that have been rubbed with a delicious spice paste,
wrapped in a banana leaf and grilled. Great party food!

SERVES 4

150 g fillet of flathead, mahi
    mahi or mackerel
1 tomato, diced
2 tbsp coconut oil
8 bay leaves
4 banana leaves
8 toothpicks

SPICE PASTE

2 pink French shallots, sliced
2 garlic cloves, sliced
1 long red chilli, sliced
1 tsp white pepper
1 tsp coriander seeds
2-cm piece of galangal, grated
1 tbsp ginger, grated
1 tbsp turmeric, ground or grated fresh
1 tbsp candlenuts or macadamias

Cut the fish into 8 even pieces. Set aside.

In a mortar and pestle (or food processor), pound
together all the spice paste ingredients until they become
smooth. Put the paste in a separate bowl and stir in the
fish, tomato pieces and oil.

Cut the banana leaves into eight 15-cm square pieces.
Place a bay leaf on the bottom, then add a piece of fish.
Wrap them by folding down the top and tucking in the
sides. Secure with a toothpick. Place on the barbie, grill
or steam. They should take about 5 minutes to cook.

Mung Bean Fritters (GF, V)

The lentils I like to use in this recipe are sometimes called 'mung dal' –
meaning the lentils (dal) have been shelled and split, thus making them easier on
our digestive tract. Any split lentil will work. You should start this recipe a day ahead.
Leave out the yoghurt for a dairy-free and vegan alternative.

MAKES 16

2 cups split mung beans, soaked
   overnight
1 tbsp garam masala
1 tbsp cumin seeds, toasted and
   ground in a mortar and pestle
1 tbsp dried chilli flakes
1 cup chopped potatoes (white or
   sweet), steamed until just tender
1 cup roughly chopped coriander
   stems and leaves
1 tbsp sea salt or tamari, or to taste
1 cup brown rice flour
1 tbsp rice bran oil
Eggplant Pickles (*see* page 171)
1 cup plain yoghurt

Drain the mung beans in a colander, then squeeze out
as much water as you can. Put them in a food processor
with the spices, chilli flakes, potato, coriander and salt
or tamari. Blitz until fairly smooth. Taste for seasoning.

Shape the mung bean mixture into 16 patties about
5 cm in diameter, then dust in the flour.

Heat the oil in a large frying pan over medium to high
heat. Shallow fry the fritters until golden on both sides.
Drain on paper towel and serve with the pickles and
yoghurt.

Smoked Trout and Feta Mousse with Corn Bruschetta (GF)

There are so many dips and spreads available now in supermarkets, and while some are okay, so many of them are not even worth considering. They contain far too much refined salt, sugar, processed ingredients and preservatives. This recipe is one you'll come back to over and over. I do.

SERVES 8

2 cups filleted and flaked smoked
  trout
½ cup crumbled goat's feta
2 tbsp capers, rinsed and squeezed dry
grated zest of 2 lemons
2 tbsp lemon juice
4 spring onions, finely chopped
2 tbsp chopped fresh dill
2 tbsp chopped flat-leaf parsley
4 anchovy fillets
1 tsp white pepper
2 lemons, quartered
corn sourdough bread
olive oil

Place the trout, feta, capers, lemon zest and juice, spring onions, herbs, anchovies and pepper in a blender and process until fairly smooth.

Heat a chargrill pan and brush both sides of the bread with a little oil. Toast over medium to high heat, until bar marks appear. Flip and repeat on the other side.

Serve with the lemon wedges.

Nori Rolls with Tempeh, Millet and Avocado
(DF, GF, V, VG)

I love making nori rolls because they are so easy to put together, are loaded
with minerals and vitamins, and they never let me down on taste. Adding the tempeh,
millet and tahini gives them a nutty flavour that goes beautifully with the ginger.
And you're getting a healthy amount of protein, calcium, iodine and iron in one dish.
You can grill the tempeh instead of shallow-frying if you like.

MAKES 4 LONG ROLLS

1 cup millet
2½ cups filtered water
60 g tempeh, cut into 1-cm strips
⅓ cup tamari
1 tsp sesame oil
1 tbsp rice bran oil or olive oil
½ cup sesame seeds
4 nori sheets
1 Lebanese cucumber, julienned
1 carrot, julienned
1 avocado, sliced
2 spring onions, sliced in half
  lengthways

TAHINI AND GINGER DRESSING
⅓ cup hulled or unhulled tahini
  (stir the tahini before using it as
  the oil separates)
1 tbsp grated fresh ginger
juice of 1 lemon or 1 tsp umeboshi
  vinegar
water, to thin out

TO SERVE
⅓ cup tamari
½ tbsp wasabi paste
½ tsp sesame oil

To cook the millet, place the millet in a saucepan and wash well. Drain and add the water. Bring to the boil, then drop to a simmer. Put the lid half on the pan and gently cook over a medium heat until the water has almost evaporated. Taste the millet – it should be just tender. If not, add a little more water. Cover completely with the lid and remove from heat. Sit, covered, for 10–15 minutes to allow the millet to continue cooking in the steam.

Meanwhile, marinate the tempeh in the tamari and sesame oil for at least 10 minutes. Shake off any excess liquid, then cook the tempeh in batches in a large frying pan in the rice bran or olive oil, or brush with oil and grill, until golden on both sides. Cool slightly.

In a dry frying pan over medium heat, toast the sesame seeds until golden. Make sure you remove them from the pan before they burn. Cool slightly then mix through the millet.

For the tahini dressing, in a bowl, mix together the tahini, ginger and lemon juice or vinegar. Add enough water to make a thick paste, a bit like yoghurt. It will look like your mixture is curdling – keep whisking until smooth.

Mix the tahini dressing through the cooled millet. The mixture should not be too wet, so add a little bit of the tahini at a time until the consistency is right.

Lay out a nori sheet, shiny side down, on the benchtop. Place about ½ cup millet mixture on the nori and, with wet hands, press it down. Leave about a 2-cm space on the edge farthest away from you. Top with a single line of each of the tempeh, cucumber, carrot, avocado and spring onion. Roll up firmly, then cut into eight pieces, or in half. Repeat with the remaining nori sheets, millet mixture and vegetables.

Serve with a dipping sauce made up of tamari, wasabi and sesame oil.

Zucchini, Mint and Feta Fritters (GF, V)

The dried mint is such a lovely addition to these fritters. You could also try fresh and dried dill instead of the mint for a different flavour. Add triple the eggs and make this into a frittata. In this case, leave out the flour.

MAKES ABOUT 16

1 small onion, diced
1 cup diced leek
2 garlic cloves, finely chopped
4 cups grated zucchini, excess
    water squeezed out
1 cup crumbled goat's feta
½ cup finely chopped mint
1 tbsp dried mint
2 tbsp grated lemon zest
½ cup brown rice flour or besan
4 eggs
1 tbsp olive oil
plain yoghurt, to serve

In a bowl, mix together the onion, leek, garlic, zucchini, feta, chopped and dried mint, lemon zest, flour and eggs.

Heat a large frying pan over medium heat, then pour in the oil. Carefully drop about 2 tablespoons of batter per fritter into the pan and cook in batches until golden, then flip. Repeat on the second side. Drain on paper towel.

Serve each fritter with a dollop of yoghurt.

San Choi Bao (DF, GF)

If you like to keep this dish vegetarian and vegan, then leave out the fish sauce.
It's fun party food – just remember to serve it with a napkin because it's juicy.

MAKES 8

2 tbsp olive oil or rice bran oil
4 spring onions, finely chopped, or
   2 tbsp finely diced French shallots
2–4 garlic cloves, crushed
2 tbsp grated fresh ginger
2 tbsp finely chopped coriander stems
2 cups finely diced firm tofu
1 cup finely chopped green beans
2 corn cobs, kernels removed
½ cup water chestnuts, diced
1–2 tbsp tamari
1 tbsp fish sauce
1–2 tbsp kecap manis (optional)
½ tbsp sesame oil
1 cup coriander leaves
1 cup bean sprouts
1 tsp dried chilli flakes (optional)
8 iceberg lettuce leaves
⅓ cup toasted sesame seeds

Heat a wok over high heat, add the olive or rice bran oil, spring onions or shallots, garlic, ginger and coriander stems. Toss for 30 seconds, add the tofu and stir-fry until the tofu starts to change colour. Toss in the beans, corn and water chestnuts and stir. Now add the sauces and sesame oil and stir-fry for a few seconds until all the ingredients are combined. Turn off the heat and stir in the coriander leaves, bean sprouts and chilli flakes (if using).

Fill each of the lettuce leaves with some of the tofu mixture, then sprinkle with the sesame seeds. Serve in these lettuce cups so each person can roll their own.

Crab and Corn Cakes (DF, GF)

I use potatoes in this recipe because, frankly, these little cakes need the starch (anything in moderation). See if you can get lovely crab claw meat in a tub from your fishmonger, rather than using the canned stuff, although it is an acceptable alternative.

MAKES 16 LITTLE CAKES

4 cups peeled and roughly chopped starchy potatoes
4 garlic cloves, crushed
4 anchovy fillets
8 spring onions, white part finely chopped (green part reserved and chopped for garnish)
1 tbsp coriander stems, thinly sliced
4 tbsp olive oil
2 corn cobs, kernels removed
1 cup coriander leaves, roughly chopped, plus extra to garnish
1 tbsp fish sauce, or to taste
zest of 2 limes
4 eggs
2 tsp cracked white pepper
1 cup flour (amaranth, besan, brown rice)
600 g fresh picked crab claw meat
2 limes, quartered

AIOLI
1 cup soy mayonnaise
1 garlic clove, peeled
2 anchovy fillets
1 spring onion
grated zest and juice of 1 lime

Steam the potatoes until tender. Set aside to cool.

For the aioli, place the mayo in a bowl. Make a paste out of the garlic, anchovies and spring onion by finely chopping the ingredients together or by roughly chopping them then pounding in a mortar and pestle. Add the paste, lime zest and juice to the mayo. Taste and adjust if necessary. Set aside.

Meanwhile, make a paste out of the garlic, anchovies, spring onions and coriander stems by pounding in a mortar and pestle or blitzing with a hand blender.

Place the paste in a frying pan over medium heat with about 1 tablespoon of the oil. Cook for 30 seconds, until fragrant, then add the corn and cook until the colour of the corn deepens, about 1 minute. Transfer to a bowl and add the coriander leaves, fish sauce, lime zest, eggs, pepper and flour. Using a fork, mash everything together until combined and fairly lump free. Gently stir in the crabmeat. The mixture will be a little wet.

Heat a large frying pan over medium to high heat, add a little of the oil and about 2 tablespoons of the mixture for each cake. Cook in batches for about 1 minute, until golden brown, then flip and cook for another minute. Repeat for the rest of the mixture and drain on paper towel.

Serve the crab and corn cakes on a platter with the aioli in a small bowl. Garnish with extra coriander leaves, the green part of the spring onions and the lime wedges.

Eggplant and Zucchini Rolls with Sunflower Seed Pesto and Bocconcini (GF)

A wonderfully colourful appetiser for a barbecue, but really these rolls are
so easy and tasty that you'll find you'll make them often. Try goat's cheese
instead of the bocconcini or leave the cheese out altogether if you're avoiding dairy.

MAKES ABOUT 16 DOUBLE ROLLS

2 large eggplants, sliced lengthways
    into 1-cm strips
4 zucchini, sliced lengthways into
    1-cm strips
2 tbsp olive oil
2 large buffalo mozzarella balls or
    1 cup bocconcini balls, cut or
    torn into thin strips or 1 cup of
    fresh ricotta
8 anchovies (optional)
cracked black pepper, to serve

SUNFLOWER SEED PESTO
1 cup sunflower seeds
2 cups basil leaves
2 garlic cloves
½ cup olive oil
sea salt

Put the eggplant and zucchini in a large bowl, add the
oil and toss to coat well. Cook the eggplant and zucchini
on a hot grill or in a large frying pan until golden on
both sides. Allow to cool a little.

To make the sunflower seed pesto, blitz together the
sunflower seeds, basil, garlic, oil and salt in a food
processor until fairly smooth.

Spread about ½ teaspoon of the pesto on each veggie
slice, place an anchovy (if using) on top, and follow with
a strip of cheese. Roll up each veggie slice and serve on
a platter. You may need to use a toothpick to keep the
roll together. Finish with cracked pepper.

Note: You can also layer the veggies, as we've done in the
photo. Place a slice of zucchini on a piece of eggplant,
then add the pesto, an anchovy and a strip of cheese
and roll up.

Betel Leaves with Prawns and Coconut (DF, GF)

You should be able to find betel leaves at your fruit and veg store; if not, ask them to get some in. If that isn't possible, you can use baby cos, witlof, or radicchio leaves instead.

MAKES 16 LEAVES

1 tbsp tamarind paste
2 tbsp grated coconut palm sugar
1 tbsp lime juice
1 tbsp fish sauce
1 tbsp tamari
2 tbsp dried shrimp
2 long red chillies, thinly sliced
2 cups grated carrot
4 tbsp shredded coconut
4 tbsp toasted peanuts, crushed
2 kaffir lime leaves, thinly sliced
½ cup each of mint and coriander
   leaves
16 small cooked prawns, peeled
   and deveined
16 betel leaves

Pound or blitz the tamarind paste, sugar, lime juice, fish sauce, tamari and dried shrimp in a mortar and pestle or blender until smooth.

Combine the chilli, carrot, coconut, peanuts, lime leaves, mint, coriander and prawns in a bowl and pour on the tamarind dressing.

Place the betel leaves on a large plate and top with a spoonful of the prawn and coconut mixture, pull out the prawns and place on top. To eat, fold the betel leaf edges over the filling and lightly roll up.

Scallops in the Shell with Mango Salsa (DF, GF)

These divine scallops are perfect for a summer barbie, or with cocktails
on a balmy night. Make the salsa ahead of time, then simply cook the scallops
and dollop the salsa on just before serving.

MAKES 16

2 mangoes, diced
juice of 2 limes
2 kaffir lime leaves, thinly sliced
½ cup roughly chopped coriander
    leaves
2 long red chillies, finely chopped
    (optional)
1 tbsp fish sauce
16 scallops in the shell, cleaned
2 tbsp rice bran oil or olive oil
16 betel leaves (optional)
½ tbsp macadamia oil (optional)

Make the salsa by gently tossing together the mango,
lime juice, kaffir lime leaves, coriander, chilli (if using)
and fish sauce. Put in the fridge until you are ready
to serve.

Chargrill or grill the scallops in a little rice bran or olive
oil in a pan or on the barbecue, for about 1 minute on
each side. Set aside to rest for a minute.

Line each scallop shell with a betel leaf (if you have
them), then top with a scallop. Spoon 1 teaspoon of salsa
on top, drizzle with the macadamia oil (if using) and eat
immediately.

Millet and Tofu Croquettes (DF, GF, V)

These are great party food, and are perfect for kids as well. Finger food
is usually a winner with little ones. Make your own crumbs by toasting leftover
rice bread and processing it into crumbs – or you can find rice crumbs in your health
food store. These croquettes are also great with only millet or quinoa, instead of both.
It is best to start this recipe a day ahead.

MAKES ABOUT 16

¾ cup millet
¾ cup quinoa
1½ cups cauliflower florets, cut
   into small pieces
1 litre vegetable stock
1 onion, diced
2 garlic cloves, crushed
2 tbsp olive oil
1½ cups mashed firm tofu
2 tbsp roughly chopped dill
2 tbsp roughly chopped flat-leaf
   parsley
1½ tbsp grated lemon zest
¾ cup brown rice flour or besan,
   plus extra for dusting
sea salt and cracked white pepper
2 eggs, beaten (leave out if you're
   vegan)
½ cup rice crumbs
2 cups rice bran oil
2 limes or lemons, quartered

Wash and drain the millet and quinoa and place in a large saucepan. Add the cauliflower and stock, bring to the boil, then drop to a simmer, half-covered, and cook until the liquid is absorbed and the grains and cauliflower are soft, about 15 minutes. Turn off the heat, leave the lid on the pan and allow to continue cooking in the residual heat.

Meanwhile, in a frying pan over medium heat, sauté the onion and garlic in the olive oil until the onion is translucent.

Put the cooled millet mixture in a large bowl and add the onion mixture. Mix in the tofu, herbs, lemon zest and flour. Taste for seasoning. Refrigerate overnight or at least for a few hours. This will make the millet mixture firmer – a bit like mashed potato.

Use about 2 tablespoons of the millet mixture for each croquette and shape into logs. Carefully dust with extra flour, dip into the eggs, then roll in the rice crumbs. (If leaving out the eggs, also omit the flour. Simply coat with the rice crumbs.)

Heat the rice bran oil in a large frying pan over high heat. Shallow-fry the croquettes in batches until golden all over. Drain on paper towel.

Serve the croquettes with the lime or lemon wedges.

DRESSINGS, DIPS AND SAUCES

Knowing how to make your own condiments is an important part of knowing how to cook healthy and tasty food well. They add flavour to otherwise bland food, and when you're first learning to cook wholefoods, this is essential. Each one of these recipes can be used in so many different ways.

MEXICAN CORN SALSA

AVOCADO DRESSING

TAHINI TARTARE

PINEAPPLE DRESSING

BEETROOT AND ALMOND DIP

CASHEW, COCONUT AND CORIANDER SAUCE

PUMPKIN HUMMUS

MINT CHUTNEY

OLIVE TAPENADE

GREEN SALSA

MUSHROOM AND WALNUT STUFFING

WHITE BEAN AND PISTACHIO DIP

MEXICAN BLACK BEAN DIP

DATE SAUCE

ZAATAR

THE PEOPLE WHO CAN MOST SUCCESSFULLY LOSE WEIGHT AND MAINTAIN A HEALTHY LIFE STYLE ARE FOODIES. WHEN IT COMES TO HEALTHY EATING, PEOPLE WHO KNOW HOW TO COOK AND MAKE INGREDIENTS TASTE GOOD HAVE A DISTINCT ADVANTAGE OVER THOSE WHO CAN'T. – EDWARD UGEL

Mexican Corn Salsa
(DF, GF, V, VG)

For a short cut, simply steam the corn instead of barbecuing it.

MAKES 1½ CUPS

2 corn cobs, husk on
¼ red onion, diced
1 tsp smoked paprika
1 tsp ground cumin
1 tomato, diced
½ cup roughly chopped
   coriander leaves
⅓ cup lemon or lime juice
½ tsp sea salt

WET PASTE
2 tbsp olive oil
1 tsp sea salt
½ cup roughly chopped
   coriander

To make the wet paste, in a bowl, combine the oil, salt and chopped coriander.

Pull the husks down over the kernels, leaving the husk attached to the bottom of the cob. Remove the silk. Using a pastry brush, dab the paste on the corn kernels. Pull the husks back over the kernels and twist the tops. You may need to use string to secure the husks.

Place the corn on a hot barbie and cook, turning a few times, for about 10 minutes, or until tender. Remove the husks, then cut off the kernels with a sharp knife and toss with the remaining ingredients.

This will last in an airtight container in the fridge for at least a few days. Serve it with raw veggie sticks, rice crackers, in a wrap, tossed through baked or steamed veggies or as a side with your piece of protein.

Avocado Dressing
(DF, GF, R, V, VG)

Try apple cider vinegar instead of lime juice for a different flavour. Both are good.

MAKES 1 CUP

1 avocado, halved
1 garlic clove, peeled
juice of 1 lime
1 tsp sea salt
filtered water

Remove the flesh from the avocado and put in a food processor along with the garlic, lime juice and salt. Blitz until smooth. You may need to adjust the consistency by adding a little water. The dressing should be thin enough to pour over steamed veggies such as squash, carrots or potato.

Store in an airtight container in the fridge – it will last a day or two.

Note: Add ½ tsp each of dried spices like cumin and paprika and/or garam masala for a curried sauce, or tamari and ginger for an Asian flavour.

Tahini Tartare (GF, V)

I make this sauce to complement seafood and once you make it the first
time it won't be long before you make it again. Use it as a spread on wraps,
nori rolls, with roast veggies, or chargrilled organic fish.

MAKES 1½ CUPS

¼ cup hulled tahini (stir the tahini
  before using it as the oil separates)
1 cup plain yoghurt
zest and juice of 1 lemon
1 garlic clove, crushed
½ tsp sea salt
½ tsp white pepper
1 tbsp capers, rinsed, squeezed dry
  and chopped
1 tbsp chopped dill pickles

Whisk together the tahini, yoghurt, lemon zest and
juice, garlic and salt. You may need to add a little more
juice or some water to thin the sauce if it is very thick.
Stir in the pepper, capers and dill pickles.

Store in a jar in the fridge for 3–4 days.

Pineapple Dressing
(DF, GF, R, V, VG)

I realise this may seem a little weird, but try it over any salad, as a marinade
for seafood (calamari loves it) or as a dressing for steamed veggies.

MAKES 2 CUPS

1 pineapple
1 tbsp olive oil
½ tbsp agave or rice syrup
1 garlic clove, peeled
½–1 tsp sea salt

Using a sharp knife, remove the skin from the pineapple,
then cut out the core.

Cut the pineapple into rough chunks, then blend with
the other ingredients until fairly smooth. Adjust the
seasoning to your taste.

Store in an airtight container in the fridge for up to
1 week.

Beetroot and Almond Dip
(DF, GF, V, VG)

The type of tahini you use will make quite a bit of difference to the taste of this richly coloured dip. 'Unhulled' means the outside husk of the sesame seed is still intact. It has more fibre and a much stronger taste than hulled tahini. Try them both and decide for yourself which you like best.

SERVES 4/MAKES 2 CUPS

4 baby beetroot, washed and trimmed
¼ cup hulled or unhulled tahini
  (stir the tahini before using it as
  the oil separates)
¼ cup whole almonds
¼ cup lemon juice
1 tsp sea salt
1 tsp almond oil

Put the beetroot in a saucepan and cover with water. Simmer for about 20 minutes, or until the beetroot are tender – test by piercing with a knife. Drain. Allow the beetroot to cool slightly, then, under the running tap, rub the skin off with your fingers.

In a food processor or blender, blitz the beetroot with the tahini, almonds, lemon juice and salt until fairly smooth. Scoop into a bowl and drizzle with the almond oil.

This is great with crudités. Store in an airtight container in the fridge for up to 1 week.

Cashew, Coconut and Coriander Sauce (DF, GF, R, V, VG)

There are so many uses for this creamy delight. Purée it with steamed veggies for a dip, use it instead of a white sauce in a veggie pie, try it as an alternative to hummus, mix it though a curry before serving, or dollop on barbecued scallops.

MAKES ABOUT 2 CUPS

1 cup raw cashew nuts, soaked for 10 minutes
1 cup roughly chopped coriander leaves and stems
½ cup flaked coconut, soaked for 10 minutes
1 tbsp lime juice
½–1 tsp sea salt

Drain the nuts, then blend with the other ingredients to form a thick paste. You may need to add a little water.

Store in an airtight container in the fridge for up to 1 week.

Pumpkin Hummus (DF, GF, V, VG)

Adding different ingredients to hummus is one of my latest experiments.
Try coriander and lime instead of the pumpkin (with or without the cumin);
rocket and mint is pretty special also. Or, for a more spicy version, simply
add 1 tablespoon of harissa paste to the basic hummus recipe.

MAKES ABOUT 3 CUPS

2 cups chopped Japanese pumpkin
400 g tin chickpeas, rinsed and
    drained
1 tbsp hulled tahini (stir the tahini
    before using it as the oil separates)
1 tbsp lemon juice
1 tsp ground cumin
1 garlic clove, finely grated
1 tsp sea salt

Steam the pumpkin until tender.

In a food processor, blitz the chickpeas until smooth,
then add the pumpkin, tahini, lemon juice, cumin, garlic
and salt and continue blitzing until combined. Adjust the
lemon juice or salt to taste.

Use for dips and breads, plus try thinning it out with
more water or lemon juice and using it as a sauce on
ravioli or in a lasagne.

It will last for at least 4 days in the fridge in an airtight
container.

Mint Chutney
(DF, GF, R, V, VG)

To make coriander chutney, simply substitute freshly
chopped coriander for the mint.

MAKES ABOUT 1 CUP

1 cup firmly packed mint leaves
2 tsp grated coconut palm sugar
   or panela
1 tsp garam masala
½ cup lime juice
1 tsp grated fresh ginger
1 long green chilli, deseeded
   and chopped
6 spring onions, chopped
1 garlic clove, crushed
sea salt, to taste
2 tbsp filtered water

Blend all the ingredients, scraping down the side of the
blender, until a smooth purée forms.

This is great with grilled fish or tofu, as a marinade,
served with fried rice or a legume salad, or you could
garnish pumpkin soup with a teaspoon or two.

Store this in a sterilised jar in the fridge for a fortnight.

Olive Tapenade
(DF, GF)

You'll be so happy you have this in the fridge. It's one of my staples, and yet another way to use olives. Leave the anchovies out to make it vego and vegan.

MAKES ABOUT 1½ CUPS

1 cup pitted black olives
1 garlic clove, peeled
1 tsp capers, rinsed and squeezed dry
6 anchovy fillets (optional)
1 tbsp each of oregano and thyme, plus extra to garnish, or 1 tsp each of dried oregano and thyme
6 sage leaves (optional)
1 tbsp dijon mustard
1 tsp cracked black pepper
½ cup extra virgin olive oil

Place all the ingredients in a food processor, or use a hand-held blender, and process until fairly smooth.

To serve, sprinkle with a few oregano and thyme leaves, if using.

Dollop it onto some freshly steamed artichokes, fresh tomatoes, through pasta, in a pie, on a wrap, as a dip or spread, or to complement your grilled protein.

This will last for weeks in the fridge.

Green Salsa (DF, GF)

I really love this salsa. It's fresh, so good for you and super tasty. There's quite a bit of salt in it from the capers, dill pickles, olives and anchovies, so you probably won't need to add any more. Have it on the table at meal or snack times, and you'll find it goes with almost everything. Omit the anchovies to make it vego and vegan.

MAKES ABOUT 3 CUPS

1 cup finely shredded mint leaves
1 cup thinly sliced basil
1 cup finely chopped coriander leaves
2 spring onions, finely chopped
1 tbsp chopped capers
4 dill pickles or gherkins, diced
½ cup green olives, pitted and diced
½ tbsp apple cider, umeboshi or
   white wine vinegar
1 tbsp olive oil (optional)
1–2 garlic cloves, finely chopped
   (optional)
2–3 anchovy fillets, chopped
   (or none)
sea salt (optional)

In a large bowl, mix everything together. Adjust seasoning to your liking.

Store in the fridge for a couple of days. It doesn't hold up very well after this as the greens will discolour, leaving it looking a little brown.

Mushroom and Walnut Stuffing
(DF, GF, V, VG)

I was blown away when I first tasted this. It's really good. Try it wrapped
in cabbage or spinach rolls, as a filling for crepes, as a dip, a sauce for pasta
or lasagne, or as a spread on your wrap.

MAKES ABOUT 2 CUPS

2 cups mushrooms, cooked in ¼ cup
   vegetable stock until softened
½ cup walnuts, roughly chopped
½ cup mashed firm tofu
1 tbsp soy milk (more if you're
   making a sauce)
½ tsp each of sea salt and cracked
   white pepper
1 small handful of basil leaves,
   roughly chopped

Purée everything together. Keep it a little chunky.

Store in the fridge for a few days.

White Bean and Pistachio Dip (DF, GF, V, VG)

The idea of this dip is to open your mind to other alternatives.
Try any bean, nut, herb or milk (just not cow's milk).

MAKES ABOUT 1½ CUPS

400 g tin navy beans, rinsed
    and drained
½ cup raw unsalted pistachio
    nuts, roughly chopped
½ cup mint leaves
2 tsp lemon zest
⅓ cup soy milk
1 tsp sea salt

Purée all the ingredients together until smooth.

Serve with crackers, carrot sticks or as a spread on wraps.

Store in an airtight container in the fridge for up to
1 week.

Mexican Black Bean Dip
(DF, GF, V, VG)

Here's a dip with a massive hit of protein thanks to the addition of both the black beans and the tofu. It's pretty delicious as well. Great also as a spread, or as a sauce over brown rice.

MAKES ABOUT 1½ CUPS

1 onion, diced
1 tbsp olive oil
2 garlic cloves, chopped
1 tsp cumin seeds, toasted and
   ground
1 tbsp chopped coriander stems
400 g tin black beans, drained
   and rinsed
1–2 jalapeño chillies
1 cup mashed firm tofu
½ cup coriander leaves
grated zest and juice of 1 lime
sea salt, to taste
4 flatbreads, toasted and broken
   into chips

Sauté the onion in the oil in a frying pan over medium heat. Add the garlic, cumin and coriander stems and stir until fragrant. Turn off the heat and add the beans, jalapeños, tofu and coriander leaves and stir to coat.

Put the onion mixture into a blender and blend until fairly smooth. Add the lime zest and juice and adjust seasoning. Serve with broken flatbread.

This dip should last in the fridge for around a week.

Date Sauce (GF, V)

This sauce tastes a little like Christmas pudding. It's really quite lovely and will lend itself to both savoury and sweet dishes.

YIELDS ABOUT 1½ CUPS

1 cup pitted and chopped dates
1 cup orange juice
1 tbsp grated orange zest
1 cup plain yoghurt

In a saucepan, soak the dates in the orange juice and zest for about 10 minutes. Bring to a simmer and cook for 10 minutes, or until the dates are soft. Let cool, then purée with the yoghurt. Refrigerate until ready to serve, or serve warm.

Serve with steamed veggies or stewed or fresh fruit.

Zaatar (DF, GF, V, VG)

This is a Middle Eastern specialty. When you're ready to eat it, mix the zaatar with 1 cup of good olive oil then either slather it all over flatbreads or crackers, coat your seafood in it, mix it through yoghurt and have as a dip, or serve it as is, in a little bowl along with olives, jalapeños and flatbread. You can experiment with other spices such as toasted ground cumin and coriander, or even a little sumac.

MAKES ABOUT 1 CUP

½ cup dried oregano
½ cup sesame seeds, toasted
1 tsp sea salt

Mix all the ingredients together and store in an airtight jar. You can blitz or pound the ingredients together for a few seconds if you'd like a smoother, more refined zaatar.

Keep the zaatar in the pantry and only add the oil to what you use. It will last for at least a month that way, even more.

SIDES AND SNACKS

It's okay to snack, but it's the type of snack we choose that's important. To truly know what's in your treats, make your own. Avoid large plastic bottles of refined oils, iodised salt, margarine, white sugar and white flour.

Spicy Macadamias

Pickled Ginger

Eggplant Pickles

Acar Acar

Olive and Rosemary Spelt Focaccia

Pickled Seaweed

Kancun

He who distinguishes the true savor of his food can never be a glutton; he who does not cannot be otherwise. ~ Henry David Thoreau

Spicy Macadamias
(DF, GF, V, VG)

I'm wary of the amount of refined salt and other undesirable ingredients
that goes into beer nuts and other packaged snacks, so I like to make my own.
Try adding sunflower seeds and pine nuts to the macas. Any nut will handle
the intense spices used here with ease.

MAKES ABOUT 1 CUP

1 cup raw unsalted macadamia nuts
1–2 tsp safflower oil or rice bran oil
1 tsp smoked paprika
1 tsp ground cumin
½–1 tsp cayenne pepper
1 tsp sea salt

Heat a frying pan over medium heat, add all the
ingredients and stir until the nuts are coated with the
spices, oil and salt, and are starting to turn golden.
Drain on paper towel and serve warm.

Pickled Ginger (DF, GF, V, VG)

Colour-free, sugar-free, preservative-free pickled ginger. The anti-inflammatory properties of ginger have been long known, so it's a good idea to eat it regularly. It's just so helpful for improving digestion, easing menstrual pain and reducing arthritic pain.

MAKES ABOUT 1 CUP

3 x 5-cm pieces of fresh ginger
½ cup sake
1 tbsp rice syrup
1 tsp sea salt

Using a vegetable peeler, take the skin off the ginger and discard. Then keep peeling so you have thin shavings of ginger.

Bring a saucepan of water to the boil and blanch the ginger for 30 seconds. Drain, then squeeze out the excess liquid.

Using the same saucepan, combine the sake, rice syrup and salt and add the ginger. Mix together and allow to marinate for at least 30 minutes.

Pickled ginger will keep in a sterilised bottle in the fridge for a few weeks.

Eggplant Pickles (DF, GF, V, VG)

I know it seems excessive to have 12 cloves of garlic and 24 chillies in one recipe, but … we are making pickles. You only have a little at a time as it's salty, oily and intense. I love this recipe, and it's so yummy with Mung Bean Fritters (*see* page 128), grilled fish, curries – just about anything really.

MAKES ABOUT 4 CUPS

2 eggplants
3 tbsp sea salt
1 tbsp yellow mustard seeds
1 tbsp grated fresh ginger
12 garlic cloves
1 tbsp ground turmeric or 2 tbsp grated fresh turmeric
2 cups mustard oil
24 long green chillies, chopped
2 cups white wine vinegar
1 cup grated coconut palm sugar or panela
1 tbsp sea salt, or to taste

Chop the eggplants into bite-sized pieces and put in a glass or ceramic bowl. Sprinkle with the salt. Leave for about 4 hours, or as long as possible, then squeeze out any excess water.

In a mortar and pestle, pound the mustard seeds, ginger and garlic to a rough paste. Add the turmeric and pound again.

Heat the oil in a saucepan and fry the spice mixture for a minute. Add the eggplant, chilli, vinegar, sugar and salt. Cook over low heat until the pickles are dry and the oil splits and sits on top. This will take maybe 45 minutes. Taste for seasoning. Let cool, then store in sterilised jars. The pickles will last for a few weeks if stored in the fridge.

Acar Acar (DF, GF)

Acar is a sweet and sour pickle. It's a gorgeous condiment to have with almost anything, especially rice. The level of heat will depend on how hot your chillies are.

MAKES ABOUT 4 CUPS

1 large cucumber, cut into batons
1 cup green beans, cut into lengths
1 cup snake beans, cut into lengths
1 carrot, cut into batons
1 cup bite-sized pieces of cabbage
1 cup cauliflower florets
4 long red chillies, deseeded and thinly sliced
4 long green chillies, deseeded and thinly sliced
1 tbsp sea salt

SPICE PASTE

10 dried long red chillies, soaked in water until starting to soften, about 30 minutes
2 lemongrass stems, white part only
4-cm piece galangal, chopped
4-cm piece fresh turmeric, grated
6 candlenuts, macadamia nuts or cashew nuts
1 tsp shrimp paste
1 tbsp olive oil or rice bran oil
1 tsp sea salt
3 tbsp grated coconut palm sugar or panela

PICKLING LIQUID

3 cups white wine or apple cider vinegar
2 French shallots, peeled and halved
10 garlic cloves, peeled

Place the cucumber, green beans, snake beans and carrot in a glass or ceramic bowl. Add the cabbage, cauliflower and chillies. Add the salt, toss well, then set aside for an hour.

To make the spice paste, drain the dried chillies, place in a blender and add the lemongrass, galangal, turmeric, nuts and shrimp paste and process until a smooth paste is formed. Heat the oil in a wok over medium–high heat and fry the paste until fragrant, about 30 seconds. Season with the salt and sugar and set aside.

When the vegetables have been together for an hour, place the vinegar, shallots and garlic in a saucepan and bring to a simmer. Quickly blanch the vegetables in the pickling liquid, then drain.

Place the pickled vegetables in a bowl with the spice paste and mix thoroughly.

Acar acar will keep for a few days stored in an airtight container in the fridge.

OPPOSITE PAGE: Acar Acar (top); Eggplant Pickles (bottom)

Olive and Rosemary Spelt Focaccia
(DF, V, VG)

'Bread baking is one of those almost hypnotic businesses, like a dance from some ancient ceremony. It leaves you filled with one of the world's sweetest smells … there is no chiropractic treatment, no Yoga exercise, no hour of meditation in a music-throbbing chapel, that will leave you emptier of bad thoughts than this homely ceremony of making bread.' M.F.K. Fisher, *The Art of Eating*

SERVES 6–8

1 cup wholemeal spelt flour
1 cup spelt flour
2 tsp sea salt, plus 2 tsp extra
2 tsp fresh yeast or ½ tsp dried yeast
1½ cups warm filtered water
2 tsp dried rosemary
½ cup pitted black olives
2 tbsp olive oil
2 tbsp rosemary leaves

Combine the flours, salt, yeast, water and dried rosemary in a large bowl and mix until a soft and smooth dough forms. Knead on a lightly floured surface for 10 minutes until the dough is elastic. Alternatively, if using a food processor, fit it with a plastic blade, place these ingredients into the bowl and process until the dough forms.

Place the dough in a bowl, cover with a damp tea towel and let it rise in a warm place for half an hour.

Mix the olives into the dough and knead again for a few minutes. Return the dough to the bowl, cover and set aside to rise for about an hour, or until doubled in size.

Preheat the oven to 220°C. Grease a 24-cm baking tin with 1 tablespoon of the oil.

Knock back the dough and put into the prepared tin. Brush the remaining oil over the top, sprinkle with the extra salt and finish with the rosemary leaves. Bake for about 20 minutes. It will look golden on top and smell divine.

Pickled Seaweed
(DF, GF, V, VG)

I don't think I can write a food book without a stand-alone seaweed recipe.
Most of us don't eat nearly enough of these magical plants from the ocean.
They are packed with minerals, iodine, omega 3 oils, super health promoting
qualities, and they make for glowing skin and shiny hair. Mixing seaweed with
other wonder foods like umeboshi, ginger, daikon and vinegar just enhances
its alchemy. Use untoasted sesame seeds to keep this dish raw.

MAKES ABOUT 1 CUP

½ cup arame
½ cup wakame
1½ cups filtered water
1 cup julienned white radish (daikon)
1 tbsp grated fresh ginger
1 tbsp tamari
2 tsp umeboshi vinegar
1 tbsp rice wine vinegar
½ tsp sesame oil
1 tbsp toasted sesame seeds,
  to garnish

In a bowl, soak the arame and wakame in the water
until soft, about 3 minutes. Add the white radish, ginger,
tamari, vinegars and sesame oil and toss. Cover and leave
to marinate in the fridge until ready to eat.

Sprinkle with the sesame seeds and serve in a small bowl
as a side dish.

Kancun (DF, GF)

If you can't find kancun (Balinese water spinach), then this recipe will work
just as well with any Asian green – choy sum, bok choy, tatsoi, gai lan. I used bok choy in
the recipe shown. It's an intensely flavoursome dish, so serve it with brown rice and fish.
Leave out the fish, shrimp paste and anchovy fillets for a vegan and vegetarian option.

SERVES 4 AS A SIDE

2 garlic cloves, thinly sliced
4 red Asian shallots, thinly sliced,
   or ½ red onion, sliced
¼ cup coconut oil
1 tsp shrimp paste or 6 anchovy fillets
1 long red chilli, thinly sliced
1 bunch kancun, washed and
   trimmed

In a wok over medium heat, sauté the garlic and shallots
in the oil until they just start to change colour. Add the
shrimp paste or anchovies and chilli and toss for a few
more seconds. Now add the kancun and, using tongs or
chopsticks, toss to combine. Cover with the lid and cook
for 30–60 seconds until the kancun wilts.

Serve immediately.

SWEET
THINGS

The sweet flavour is just as necessary as all the others. There is no good reason to deprive yourself of sweets, but of course you need to choose whole, complex sweeteners instead of refined and highly processed sugars. Never feel guilty about eating the desserts in these pages – it's better for you to eat them than to not.

PISTACHIO AND ROSEWATER HALVA

CHOCOLATE PIE

TOFU MISO CHEESECAKE WITH APRICOT COULIS

CHOCOLATE CAKES WITH GANACHE FILLING

RHUBARB CRUMBLE

CHILLED MANGO AND COCONUT PUDDINGS

YOGHURT PANNA COTTA WITH POMEGRANATE AND ALMONDS

FRUIT SUNDAES

FIG AND WALNUT LOG

STEWED APPLES WITH PISTACHIO RICE CREAM

SEMOLINA PUDDING

FIG, COCONUT AND CACAO TRUFFLES

FIGS WITH ROSEWATER AND PISTACHIO YOGHURT

FRIED BANANAS WITH CHOCOLATE CASHEW CREAM

CHOCOLATE AND ORANGE MOUSSE

COCONUT AND MANGO PUDDINGS

APRICOT AND COCONUT MUESLI BARS

MAPLE NUT 'CHEESE' CAKE

CHOCOLATE ALMOND TRUFFLES

SAVE THE EARTH. IT'S THE ONLY PLANET WITH CHOCOLATE. ~ AUTHOR UNKNOWN

OPPOSITE PAGE: Maple Nut 'Cheese' Cake

Pistachio and Rosewater Halva (DF, GF, V, VG)

I love halva, but I never buy it because of the tons of white sugar in it.
Voilà! A healthy halva.

MAKES 10 SLICES

1 cup sesame seeds, toasted
2 tbsp pistachio nuts
1 tsp rosewater
2 tbsp raisins
2 tbsp agave or rice syrup

In a spice grinder or mortar and pestle, pound the sesame seeds to a fine powder.

Transfer the ground sesame seeds to a food processor, add the rest of the ingredients and process until you get a stiff batter. Spoon the mixture onto a piece of baking paper about 30 cm long and shape into a log. Roll the paper tightly around the log, twisting the ends. Refrigerate for at least an hour before eating.

Serve in the paper, opened up and cut into 2-cm rounds.

Chocolate Pie (DF, GF, R, V, VG)

Mixing cacao with avocado pretty much gives you chocolate mousse.
Fill a sweet, nutty base with it and you'll have a wonderful pie
on your table in less than an hour.

SERVES 6–8

1 cup unsalted raw nuts, any kind
1 cup desiccated or flaked coconut
½ cup dried apricots, soaked in water
   for 30 minutes
1½ cups medjool dates, pitted
3 avocados, pitted
¾ cup raw cacao powder
½ cup coconut oil
agave, to taste

For the base, process the nuts, coconut, drained dried apricots and 3 of the dates until sticky. Press into a 23-cm round flan tin. Refrigerate while you prepare the filling.

Scoop the avocado flesh into the bowl of a food processor, add the cacao powder, coconut oil and the rest of the dates and blitz until smooth. Taste; if you'd like a sweeter filling, add some agave.

Spread the filling over the base and chill for at least an hour.

Tofu Miso Cheesecake
with Apricot Coulis (DF, V, VG)

I like the addition of miso in this recipe. It gives a deep, rich flavour. The tofu and kudzu act as setting agents, so you can be sure the filling will be firm once it's cooled.

SERVES 8

BASE
3 cups spelt flour, plus extra
    for dusting
1 tsp ground cinnamon
½ tsp sea salt
½ cup safflower oil
½ cup chilled filtered water
1 tbsp maple syrup

APRICOT COULIS
6 fresh apricots, stones removed,
    roughly chopped
1 tbsp grated coconut palm sugar
    or panela

FILLING
500 g silken tofu
400 g firm tofu
1 cup maple syrup
½ cup kudzu
2 tbsp sunflower oil or safflower oil
zest and juice of 1 lemon
2 tbsp lemon juice, extra
2 tbsp shiro miso
1 vanilla bean, split in half lengthways
    and seeds scraped, or 1 tsp natural
    vanilla extract
1 tsp low-allergy baking powder

Preheat the oven to 180°C. Lightly brush a 25-cm tart tin with a removable base with a little oil.

For the base, in a large bowl, combine the dry ingredients. Using a spoon, mix in the oil, then slowly add the water and the maple syrup. Bring together to form a sticky and slightly oily dough, then knead on a lightly floured surface for 5 minutes. Shape into a ball, cover with plastic wrap and chill for 30 minutes.

Dust the pastry with a little spelt flour and roll out to about 3 mm thick. Press the pastry into the base of the tin. Line the pastry shell with a piece of baking paper and pour in some baking beads, uncooked rice or dried legumes. Blind bake for 10 minutes. Remove the paper and beads and allow the pastry to cool.

Blend the apricots until smooth, then pour them into a pan over a medium heat and add the sugar. Gently simmer for about 5 minutes until the sugar is dissolved, stirring regularly. Cool and refrigerate until you're ready to serve the cake.

For the filling, blend all the ingredients until smooth and creamy. Pour the tofu mixture onto the baked pastry base and bake for 1 hour, or until the filling is set around the edges and almost set in the centre, and the top begins to brown. Allow to cool slightly, then run a small sharp knife around the sides to loosen the cheesecake from the tin. Cool completely, then cover with plastic wrap and refrigerate for at least 4 hours.

Release the cheesecake from the tin and place on a serving plate. Serve with the apricot coulis.

Chocolate Cakes with Ganache Filling (DF, V, VG)

Biting into these little cakes and getting a mouthful of chocolate ganache is pretty nice. Serve these warm with some soy ice cream. You can grease the muffin tin with coconut oil for a delicious change, and serve the cakes with coconut soy ice cream.

MAKES 6 SMALL CAKES

GANACHE

200 g dark chocolate, roughly chopped
½ cup soy or almond milk

CAKES

1½ cups spelt flour
½ cup unsweetened cocoa powder (or raw cacao powder)
1 tsp low-allergy baking powder
½ tsp bicarbonate of soda
pinch of sea salt
120 g silken tofu
¾ cup soy milk
¾ cup agave or maple syrup
½ cup sunflower oil
2 tsp natural vanilla extract

TO SERVE

unsweetened cocoa powder (or raw cacao powder), sifted
vanilla soy ice cream
mixed berries

For the ganache, place a heatproof bowl over a saucepan of simmering water. (Make sure the bottom of the bowl doesn't touch the water.) Turn off the heat, place the chocolate in the bowl and stir until melted. Beat in the milk until smooth. Cover with plastic wrap and refrigerate until firm.

Preheat the oven to 180°C. Grease six holes in a standard muffin tin.

For the cakes, in a large bowl, sift the flour, cocoa (or cacao), baking powder and bicarbonate of soda with the salt. Mix well. In a food processor, blend the tofu, milk, syrup of your choice, oil and vanilla. Pour the wet ingredients into the dry and mix to combine.

Half fill the prepared muffin holes with the cake mixture. Place 1–2 tablespoons of ganache on top, then spoon in more cake mixture to fill each hole. Bake for 15 minutes, or until the cakes are firm to touch and pull away from the side of the tin.

Dust with the cocoa (cacao) powder and serve with the ice cream and some scattered berries.

Rhubarb Crumble (VG)

Crumbles are traditionally made with butter and sugar. Naturally, this one isn't.
I don't think you need to add these things to get a really sweet dessert. Not
when you've got fresh fruit and dates around. Leave out the yoghurt
to make it a dairy-free and vegan option.

SERVES 4

2 apples, cored and thinly sliced
2 pears, cored and thinly sliced
1 cup thinly sliced trimmed rhubarb
1 cup orange juice
4 dates, pitted and roughly chopped
2 cups raw rolled oats
1 cup roughly chopped whole
  almonds
1 cup pepitas
1 tbsp ground cinnamon
½ cup sunflower seeds
1 tbsp omega spread or sunflower oil
plain yoghurt, to serve (optional)

Place the fruit, orange juice and dates in a large saucepan over low heat, and put the lid half on. Stew, without stirring, until the fruit is tender, about 15 minutes.

Meanwhile, to make the topping, mix all the dry ingredients together in a large bowl. Using your hands, rub in the spread or oil until the mixture resembles chunky breadcrumbs. Set aside.

Preheat the oven to 180°C.

Spoon the stewed fruit into a 20 x 15 cm ovenproof dish and top with the crumble. Bake until the crumble just starts to change colour, about 15 minutes.

Serve with a dollop of yoghurt, if you like.

Chilled Mango and Coconut Puddings (DF, GF, V, VG)

These are a lovely little dessert. Perfect for a barbecue or picnic.
I haven't added any sweetener apart from the fruit, so feel free to add
some agave or maple syrup if your tooth is sweeter.

SERVES 4

3 mangoes, peeled and sliced
a few drops of orange blossom water
½ cup filtered water
½ cup rice flour
400 g tin coconut milk
pinch of sea salt

To Serve
2 mango cheeks
½ cup flaked coconut

Blend the mangoes with the orange blossom water. Set aside.

Bring the water to the boil in a saucepan and whisk in the flour. Lower the heat, add the milk and salt and keep whisking until the mixture thickens, only a minute or so. Remove from the heat and stir in the mango purée. Cool slightly, pour into individual glasses, cover with plastic wrap and allow to set in the fridge, about an hour.

Decorate with the mango cheeks and flaked coconut and serve.

Yoghurt Panna Cotta with Pomegranate and Almonds (GF, V)

This would also be nice using goat's yoghurt instead of sheep's yoghurt.
The jewels from the pomegranate make it look like a dessert
for a special occasion.

MAKES 4

½ cup almond milk
1 vanilla bean, split lengthways and
    seeds scraped, or ½ tsp natural
    vanilla extract
1 tbsp agar agar
1½ cups sheep's yoghurt
    (unsweetened)
1 tbsp agave
2 pomegranates, deseeded
½ cup roughly chopped whole
    almonds, toasted
mint sprigs, to serve

Place the milk and vanilla seeds in a saucepan over low heat. Stir in the agar agar and gently heat, stirring frequently, until the agar dissolves. Allow to cool, then whisk in the yoghurt, agave, half the pomegranate seeds and the almonds.

Pour the panna cotta into four individual 1-cup moulds, cover with plastic wrap and refrigerate until firm, about 1 hour.

Decorate with the mint and the rest of the pomegranate seeds and serve.

Fruit Sundaes (DF, GF, V, VG)

These sundaes are too cute. I've used mango and raspberries but any
fruit in season is lovely. Try kiwi fruit, apricots, lemons,
guava, mulberries or passionfruit.

SERVES 4

2 cups apple juice
2½ tbsp agar agar
pinch of sea salt
1 mango, chopped
1½ cups raspberries
125 g silken tofu
1 tbsp agave
1 tsp natural vanilla extract
extra raspberries, to serve

In a saucepan, combine the apple juice, agar agar and salt
over medium heat. Bring to the boil and simmer, stirring
frequently, for 10 minutes, or until the agar dissolves.
Take off the heat and set aside.

Put the mango in a bowl, 1 cup of the raspberries in
another bowl and the tofu in a third bowl, then pour
one-third of the apple juice mixture over each. Stir
the agave and vanilla into the tofu mixture to sweeten
it. Purée each mixture separately. Add the remaining
raspberries to the raspberry purée and stir to combine.

To assemble, divide the mango, tofu and raspberry
mixtures between four serving glasses. You should have
a layer of the three different mixtures in each glass. Place
in the fridge to chill. Sprinkle the top with the extra
raspberries.

Fig and Walnut Log
(DF, GF, V, VG)

This is a lovely addition to a cheese platter. Slice the log into 2-cm thick
rounds and place on a platter with grapes, goat's cheese and rice
crackers or gluten-free Essene bread.

MAKES ONE 20-CM LOG

1 cup dried figs
1 cup pitted dates
1 tsp ground cinnamon
1 cup walnuts
½ cup unsalted pistachio nuts

In a food processor, blitz together the figs, dates and
cinnamon for about 5 seconds. Then add the nuts and
briefly blitz. You don't want the nuts ground too finely;
it's nice if there are still some chunks.

Place the fig mixture on some baking paper and shape
into a log about 5 cm thick. Roll the paper round the
log, twist the ends and put in the fridge to harden a
little. This should take about an hour.

Leave it in the paper in the fridge and it will last for
ages – at least a month.

Stewed Apples with Pistachio Rice Cream (DF, GF, V, VG)

You'll be so excited to taste this rice cream, and even happier to know
you can make it quickly and easily at home. Try different ingredients
to flavour it – such as orange water and raw cacao powder,
mango and kaffir lime, or coffee and hazelnuts.

SERVES 4

½ cup unsalted pistachio nuts,
   chopped
2 cups rice milk, frozen
1 tsp rosewater
1 tbsp agave
4 granny smith apples
3 dried figs
1 tbsp grated orange zest
pinch of saffron threads
1 cinnamon stick
small piece of orange zest
4 mint sprigs, to serve

Grind the pistachios in a spice or coffee grinder or
pound in a mortar and pestle.

In a food processor or blender, combine the frozen milk,
rosewater, agave and ground pistachios and process until
smooth. Transfer to a bowl, cover and place in the freezer
for at least 30 minutes, until firm.

Core the apples, taking a little extra flesh from around
the core. Chop or process the figs and orange zest
together until almost smooth. Now stuff the cavity in
each apple with this mixture.

Place the apples in a large saucepan, pour in enough
water to come a third of the way up the side of the
apples, and add the saffron, cinnamon stick and orange
zest. Half cover with the lid and steam until tender,
about 20 minutes (or place in an ovenproof dish and
bake for 30 minutes at 180°C until tender when pierced
with a skewer). Take the apples out of the liquid and
simmer the liquid until reduced a little. Remove the
cinnamon stick, reserve, and discard the orange peel.

To serve, spread some pistachio rice cream in a shallow
bowl, place an apple on top and drizzle with some of the
cooking liquid. Decorate with a piece of the cinnamon
stick and a sprig of mint.

Semolina Pudding
(DF, V)

Spreading a wet dessert like this on a platter is a lovely way to serve it.
Have a few spoons resting on the edges and let your guests or family help themselves.
This pudding is quite sweet, so you may want to cut down on the sugar or honey.

SERVES 6

5 cups filtered water
1 cup grated coconut palm sugar
    or panela
½ cup raw honey
1 slice of lemon peel
3 cinnamon sticks
2 whole cloves
1 cup safflower oil
2 cups coarse semolina
¼ cup raisins
¼ cup pine nuts, plus extra to garnish
¼ cup crushed walnuts
½ cup passionfruit pulp
1 tbsp agave
zest of 1 lemon or orange

In a large saucepan, mix together the water, sugar, honey, lemon peel, cinnamon and cloves and boil gently for 1 minute. Add the oil, then, whisking constantly, slowly pour in the semolina and continue whisking for about 2 minutes over a low heat. Once thick, add the raisins, pine nuts and walnuts and keep stirring until the semolina is cooked, about 5 minutes. You may need to add some water to get it to the desired consistency. It should be easy to pour.

Spoon the semolina pudding onto a platter and cover with the passionfruit pulp, agave and zest.

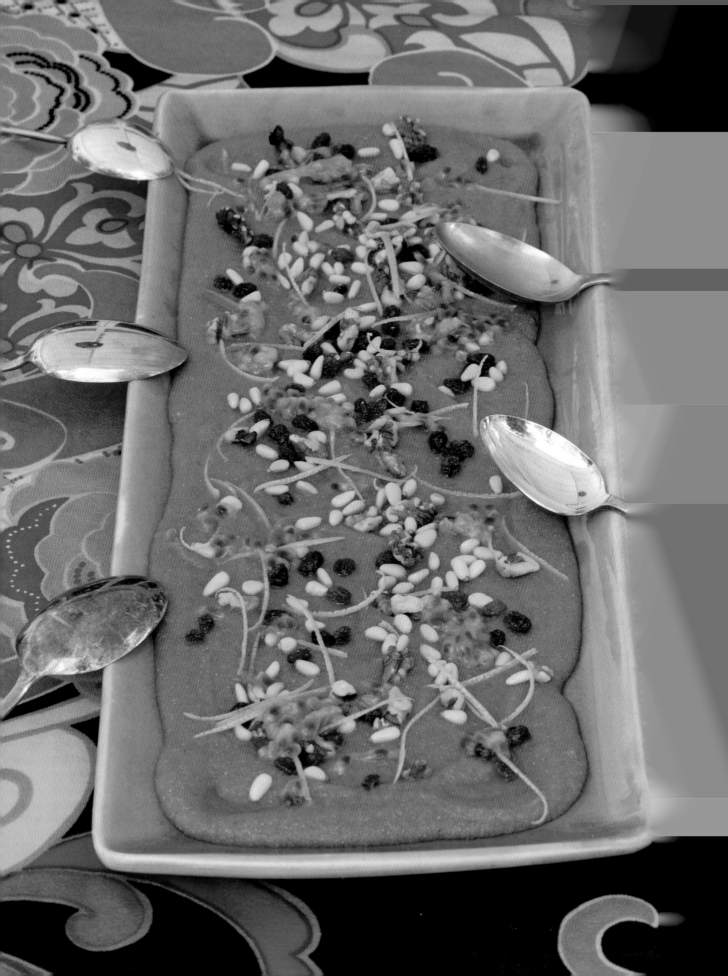

Fig, Coconut and Cacao Truffles (DF, GF, R, V, VG)

I love making little balls of goodness like these. You can use whatever
dried fruit and nuts you have in the cupboard, and experiment with different spices.
Sometimes I add seeds, LSA, spirulina or barley grass powder.

MAKES ABOUT 20

1 cup roughly chopped dried figs
1 cup pitted and roughly chopped
   dates
1 cup desiccated coconut, plus extra
   for dusting
½ cup walnuts, chopped
½ cup raw cacao powder
½ tsp ground cardamom
1 tsp lemon zest
½–¾ cup coconut oil
2 tbsp each extra raw cacao powder
   or ground walnuts, for dusting

Place the dried fruit in the food processor and process to
a chunky paste. Add the rest of the ingredients, leaving
the oil until last. Blitz until smooth and glossy.

Roll the mixture into balls the size of a walnut, then dust
in the extra cacao powder or ground walnuts.

These will keep for months stored in an airtight
container in the pantry. Chill if you like a firmer treat.

Figs with Rosewater and Pistachio Yoghurt (GF, V)

This is one of those wonderful desserts that you can make
and assemble in a few minutes, yet it looks so impressive.

SERVES 4

2 tbsp grated coconut palm sugar
  or panela
4 figs
1 tbsp rice bran oil or omega spread
½ cup unsalted pistachio nuts
1 tbsp linseeds
4 tbsp plain yoghurt
1 tsp rosewater
4 mint leaves

Sprinkle the sugar on a plate. Cut the figs in half then
press the cut side into the sugar. Barbecue or pan-fry in
the oil or spread until golden brown.

Meanwhile, separately grind the pistachios and linseeds.

In a small bowl, mix together the yoghurt, rosewater and
pistachios.

To serve, place the figs on a platter, some facing up and
some down. Dollop the yoghurt over the figs, sprinkle
with the ground linseeds and decorate with the mint.

Fried Bananas with Chocolate Cashew Cream (DF, GF, V, VG)

The chocolate cashew cream is sheer heaven. Add 1 teaspoon
of coconut oil and you'll wonder why you ever ate dairy.

SERVES 4

½ cup raw unsalted cashew nuts
½ cup soy or almond milk
1 tsp unsweetened cocoa powder or
  raw cacao powder
2 tbsp omega spread or rice bran oil
4 bananas, peeled and sliced in half
  lengthways
1 tbsp grated orange zest

In a food processor, process the cashews, milk and cocoa
or cacao until you have a creamy sauce. Add more milk if
it's too thick.

Heat a non-stick frying pan over medium heat and
soften the omega spread or heat the oil. Fry the bananas
on each side for about 1 minute, or until starting to turn
golden.

To serve, pour the cashew cream over the bananas and
sprinkle on the orange zest.

Chocolate and Orange Mousse
(DF, GF, R, V, VG)

It continues to surprise me just how unnecessary dairy, white sugar
and refined white flour are, even when making desserts. This is a wonderfully
sensual mousse. Serve it with an orange segment, a nasturtium
or another edible flower you love.

MAKES 6

½ cup pitted dates, soaked in orange
  juice for a couple of hours
3 avocados, pitted
100 g unsweetened cocoa powder
¼ cup agave, or to taste
1 tsp tamari, or to taste
1 tsp ground cinnamon (optional)
1 tsp natural vanilla extract
2 tbsp grated orange zest, plus extra
  to serve
coconut cream or milk, to serve
  (optional)

Drain the dates, then roughly chop.

Place the dates in a blender or food processor, add
the avocado flesh, cocoa, agave, tamari, cinnamon and
vanilla and blend until smooth. Half-fill individual
½-cup moulds and chill for about an hour.

Serve with the coconut cream or milk (if using) and
the extra orange zest.

Coconut and Mango Puddings
(DF, GF, R, V)

I've used mango here (because I love it) but experiment with other fruits.
Almost any will work. It's great how the lecithin sets the puddings,
and it's great to help reduce elevated cholesterol.

SERVES 6

400 ml tin coconut milk
2 cups mango flesh
½ cup raw honey, or agave or maple
  syrup if vegan
200 g lecithin granules (non GM)
juice of 1 lime
zest of 2 limes

Blend the coconut milk, half the mango, the sweetener, lecithin, lime juice and half the lime zest until smooth. Pour into six 1-cup capacity moulds, cover and put in the fridge to set until firm, about 4 hours.

Purée the remaining mango with the remaining lime zest and serve with the puddings.

Apricot and Coconut Muesli Bars
(DF, V)

Commercially produced muesli bars are often full of processed
sugar and milk powder. And just as worrying or maybe even worse,
dried fruit that's been preserved with sulphur dioxide. Make your own –
it's more economical and they taste so much better.
Plus you feel like the baking queen.

MAKES ABOUT 20 BARS

1 cup rolled oats
1 cup desiccated coconut
½ cup wheat germ
½ cup sesame seeds
½ cup sunflower seeds
½ cup pepitas
½ cup ground linseeds or LSA
1 cup organic dried apricots, roughly
   chopped (or any dried fruit will do)
1 cup coconut oil
1 cup raw honey or rice syrup
1 cup hulled tahini (stir the tahini
   before using it as the oil separates)

Preheat the oven to 180°C. Grease and line a 30-cm
square baking tin.

In a large saucepan, toast the rolled oats, coconut, wheat
germ, sesame and sunflower seeds and pepitas until
golden. Transfer to a bowl and allow to cool. Add the
ground linseeds or LSA.

Transfer the oat mixture to a food processor, add the
dried apricots and, with the motor running, pour in the
coconut oil, honey or rice syrup, and tahini. Process only
until the mixture is just combined.

Using your hands or the back of a spoon, press the
mixture into the prepared tin. Mark into squares or bars
and bake for 15–20 minutes, or until golden. Turn onto
a wire rack to cool completely.

These bars will keep in an airtight container for months.

Maple Nut 'Cheese' Cake
(DF, GF, R, V, VG)

This is my favourite dessert at the moment and I wonder if I will ever tire of it.
The soaking liquid from the nuts is full of nutrients so don't throw it away.
Either drink it yourself or give your plants a little drink.

BASE

1 cup each of unsalted walnuts and
  Brazil nuts, soaked in filtered water
  overnight
4 dates, soaked in 1½ cups filtered
  water for a few hours
½ tsp freshly grated nutmeg

FILLING

3 cups cashew nuts, soaked in filtered
  water overnight, then drained
150 ml maple syrup
1 tbsp psyllium husks
1 tbsp lecithin granules (non GM)
juice of 1 lemon
1 vanilla bean, split in half lengthways
  and seeds scraped
grated zest of 2 lemons
pinch of sea salt
150 ml coconut oil

MANGO COULIS

2 cups mango flesh, blended

For the base, drain the nuts and dates, reserving the
soaking liquid from the dates. Combine the nuts, dates
and nutmeg in a food processor and blitz until smooth.
Press into the base of a 23-cm springform cake tin. Chill
for at least 10 minutes while you are preparing the filling.

For the filling, place the soaking liquid from the dates
in a blender or food processor, add the other ingredients
and blend until smooth. Pour over the base. Chill until
set, about an hour or so but better overnight.

Serve the cake with the mango coulis.

Chocolate Almond Truffles
(DF, GF, V, VG)

These truffles are one of those things that you'll make often. Perfect at the end of a dinner party, during the festive season or as a birthday gift … or just for you. This recipe needs a few hours to set, so start in the morning or the night before.

MAKES ABOUT 12

1 cup slivered almonds
1 cup chopped dark chocolate
2 tbsp omega spread
1–2 tbsp orange liqueur
raw cacao powder, for dusting
flaxseed meal, for dusting

Combine the almonds, chocolate and spread in a heatproof bowl over a saucepan of simmering water and let the chocolate melt. Stir through the orange liqueur. Cover the bowl with plastic wrap and put in the fridge overnight.

Use a teaspoon or melon baller to shape the chocolate mixture into small balls. Put the cacao powder and ground linseeds on separate plates and roll the truffles in each to coat.

Refrigerate until firm, about an hour or two. Store in an airtight container in the fridge for up to a month.

Conversion Tables

Please note that Australian spoon and cup measurements are used in this book.
All spoon and cup measurements are level, not heaped, unless otherwise indicated.

TEMPERATURES

Gas Mark	Fahrenheit	Celsius	Description
¼	225	110	Very slow
½	250	130	Very slow
1	275	140	Slow
2	300	150	Slow
3	315/325	160/170	Very moderate
4	350	180	Moderate
5	375	190	Moderately hot
6	400	200	Moderately hot
7	425	220	Hot
8	450	230	Hot
9	475	240	Very hot

LIQUID CONVERSION

Metric (approximation)	Imperial
15 ml	½ fl oz
20 ml	⅔ fl oz
30 ml	1 fl oz
60 ml	2 fl oz
125 ml	4 fl oz
150 ml	5 fl oz
175 ml	6 fl oz
250 ml	8½ fl oz
300 ml	10 fl oz (½ pint UK)
375 ml	12½ fl oz
500 ml	17 fl oz
600 ml	20 fl oz (1 pint UK)
750 ml	25 fl oz
1000 ml (1 L)	33 fl oz

Glossary

Acai powder. The Acai berry (pronounced ah-SIGH-ee) is one of nature's superfoods. It comes from an Amazon palm tree that is harvested in the rainforests of Brazil. It is full of antioxidants, amino acids and essential fatty acids. Gluten free.

Agar agar is a dried seaweed. A vegan substitute for gelatine to set desserts and some savoury dishes. It is available in flakes, powder or bars and is sometimes called Kanten. Gluten free.

Agave is a complex sweetener from the cactus of the same name. It won't send blood sugar levels up and tastes like toffee. Gluten free.

Amaranth is one of the oldest cereal varieties cultivated – this was the principal foodstuff of the Incas and Aztecs. It is extraordinarily healthy as a cereal or foliage plant because of the high protein content – 16 per cent – and its leaves are popular as either a vegetable or seasoning. Gluten free.

Apple or pear juice concentrate is a complex sweetener made from fruit. Comes as a thick syrup. Gluten free.

Arame. This seaweed contains 10 times the calcium of milk and 500 times the iodine of shellfish. Keep in the fridge soaking in water and add it to salads or stir-fries as you need it, or add it as a dried ingredient to winter casseroles, grains and soups. Gluten free.

Besan flour is made by grinding dried chickpeas. Gluten free.

Betel leaves. The betel (*Piper betle*) is the leaf of a vine belonging to the Piperaceae family, which includes pepper and kava. It is valued both as a mild stimulant and for its medicinal properties. It is cultivated in most of South and Southeast Asia. Available from good fruit and veggie stores.

Candlenuts. A nut native to South East Asia. Macadamia nuts are sometimes substituted for candlenuts when they are not available, as they have a similarly high oil content and texture when pounded. The flavour, however, is quite different, as the candlenut is much more bitter. These nuts must be toasted as they are mildly toxic if consumed raw.

Chia seeds are a tiny seed high in omega 3, protein and fibre. Part of the mint family, they are native to Mexico and Guatemala and come in different colours such as black, brown, gray and white. The seeds are gelatinous and swell once in contact with liquid, so they are good to keep blood sugar balanced as they keep you full for longer. Add them to porridge, smoothies, cereal and desserts.

Dashi is a powdered stock that consists of shiitake mushrooms, kombu and bonito (fish) flakes. There is also a vegetarian option available without the bonito. Gluten free.

Flaxseed oil (also known as linseed oil). Flaxseed oil comes from the seeds of the flax plant. It contains both omega-3 and omega-6 fatty acids, which are needed for good health.

Flaxseed oil contains the essential fatty acid alpha-linolenic acid (ALA), which the body converts into eicosapentaenoic acid (EPA) and docosahexaenoic acid (DHA), the omega-3 fatty acids found in fish oil. Gluten free.

Freekeh is made by roasting green wheat. This grain is easy to digest. Wheat, when harvested young, retains more of its proteins, vitamins and minerals and generates great health benefits. Use as you would any grain.

Galangal is related to ginger, and is similar in appearance (not taste) with its knobbly root-like form. Its skin is reddish-brown in colour and thicker than ginger, while its flesh is off-white. It has a citrusy, piney, earthy aroma, with hints of cedar and soap (saponins) in the flavour. Galangal has little of the peppery heat that raw ginger has. It is available as a whole rhizome, cut or powdered. The whole fresh rhizome is very hard, and slicing it requires a sharp knife.

Goji berries grow in temperate and subtropical regions in China, Mongolia and in the Himalayas in Tibet. They are in the nightshade (Solanaceae) family. They have been cultivated in China for more than 600 years for use in traditional Chinese medicine but have only recently become popular in the West. They are known for having an exceptionally high level of antioxidants. Goji berries are usually found dried. They are shrivelled red berries that look like red raisins.

Kale. A member of the cabbage family, kale is native to the British Isles and Eastern Mediterranean countries. There are many varieties of both curly- and smooth-leaved kale. Called *cavalo nero* in Italy, it is rich in antioxidants (some say more than any other veggie) and does not lose volume like silverbeet or spinach when cooked, but it does need to be cooked longer.

Kancun. Indonesian water spinach. Use any Asian green or kale, if you can't find it.

Kecap manis is a sweet soy sauce that is available at Asian grocery stores. It usually contains palm sugar so I avoid it. Gluten free.

Kombu is seaweed and it is an important part of Japanese cuisine. Kombu is also eaten in other parts of Asia as well; it can be found fresh, dried, pickled, and frozen in many Asian markets or supermarkets.

Korengo fronds. This is a sea vegetable rich in vitamins and minerals, including calcium, magnesium and zinc. They are bite-sized pieces of seaweed that can be used as a snack straight out of the bag or used in cooking as a garnish for various dishes.

Kudzu is related to arrowroot and is used to thicken sauces where you would use cornflour. It's also used to treat diarrhoea. Available in small rocks or a powder. Gluten free.

Linseed oil – *see* flaxseed oil above.

Lecithin granules. Lecithin is a naturally occurring fatty substance found in a variety of different foods such as soybeans, egg yolks and whole grains. It helps the body utilise certain vitamins such as vitamins A, B, E, and K. Lecithin granules also help to break down fat and cholesterol into smaller pieces.

LSA. A combination of ground linseeds (flaxseeds), sunflower seeds and almonds.

Maca powder. Maca (*Lepidium meyenii*) is a root plant from Peru consumed as a food and for medicinal purposes. It is traditionally used to increase stamina and sexual function, energy and endurance and to balance hormones. It is available as a capsule, liquid extract or powder. Maca is often touted as an aphrodisiac.

Mandoline is a cooking utensil used for slicing and for cutting juliennes.

Millet is the oldest cultivated variety of cereal in the world; this is an important basic foodstuff in Africa and Central Asia. It is rich in unsaturated fatty acids and vitamins. Gluten free.

Mirin. This Japanese sherry is commonly used in sauces and stir-fries. Gluten free.

Miso is a fermented soy product. It is used in soups and sauces and is great for balancing gut flora and any other stomach complaints. Don't boil it for too long, as boiling kills the live enzymes it contains. Generally the lighter coloured pastes like shiro are sweeter, and the darker – genmai and hatcho – are saltier and more pungent. Use the lighter pastes in the warmer weather. Gluten free.

Nori is a dried sea vegetable that comes in paper-like sheets. It can be eaten as a snack or wrapped around rice. It has the highest protein content and is the most easily digested of all the seaweeds. Garnish your vegetables or soups with shredded nori. Or use instead of flatbread for your wrap. Gluten free.

Oat meal is ground oats as opposed to whole oats or oat flakes.

Omega spread. Melrose Foods has developed an alternative to margarine and butter. The Omegacare range of table spreads is high in omega-3 and very low in saturated fat. They are not hydrogenated or heat-treated, contain minimal natural trans fats, have no cholesterol, are non-dairy, and GM free.

Panela is unrefined whole cane sugar, typical of Latin America. It is a solid piece of sucrose and fructose obtained from boiling and evaporating sugarcane juice. Also known as rapadura.

Pepitas. This is the inside part of the pumpkin seed. High in zinc and fibre.

Pomegranate molasses is made by boiling down the juice of a tart variety of pomegranate. It forms a thick, dark brown liquid that is used in dressings and pilafs.

Psyllium seed husks are portions of the seeds of the plant *Plantago ovata*, a native of India. They are hygroscopic (that is, they absorb water, expanding and become mucilaginous). They are recommended for colon cleansing/ bowel regulation as well as for better blood circulation. Psyllium seed husk are indigestible and are a source of soluble dietary fiber. They are used to relieve constipation, irritable bowel syndrome, and diarrhoea. Some recent research is also showing them to be promising in lowering cholesterol and controlling diabetes. Gluten free.

Quark is a type of fresh cheese. It is made by warming soured milk until the desired degree of de-naturation of milk proteins is met, and then it is strained. Traditional quark is not made with rennet. It is soft, white and unaged, similar to some types of fromage frais. It is distinct from ricotta because ricotta is made from scalded whey. Quark usually has no salt added and is known for its beneficial effect on the digestive system. Gluten free.

Quinoa. This herb grows in the Andes at altitudes in excess of 4000 metres, and its small seeds are rich in vitamins and nutrients.

It is used in the same way as grains, and was much prized by the Incas. Gluten free.

Raw cacao powder. Cacao (pronounced ka-kow) beans are the seeds of an Amazonian fruiting tree and the source of all chocolate and cocoa products. As the temperature during processing is never allowed to exceed 40°C, the powder is considered a 'raw' food with all heat-sensitive vitamins, minerals and antioxidants remaining intact, thereby maximising digestion and absorption. It has over 360 per cent more antioxidants than regular cocoa. Gluten free.

Raw honey is the concentrated nectar; it is unheated, pure, unpasteurised and unprocessed. An alkaline-forming food, this type of honey contains ingredients similar to those found in fruits, which become alkaline in the digestive system. Gluten free.

Rapadura – *see* Panela

Rice syrup a complex sweetener with the consistency of honey, but not as sweet. It is made by pounding brown rice. Gluten free.

Sake is an alcoholic beverage of Japanese origin that is made from fermented rice. Sake is often referred to as a form of rice wine. However, unlike wine, in which alcohol is produced by fermenting the sugar naturally present in grapes, sake is produced by means of a brewing process similar to brewing beer. It is more like rice beer than rice wine.

Sambal oelek. A paste made from ground red chillis, sometimes including salt, lime or lemongrass. Used for adding heat to dishes without altering the other flavours. Sambal oelek can be made from raw ingredients or purchased ready made.

Semolina the centre part of durum wheat obtained after processing and separating it. When mixed with flour it becomes couscous. It's used to make puddings and other desserts, pasta and breakfast cereals. Contains gluten.

Shaoxing rice wine is one of the most famous varieties of traditional Chinese wines fermented from rice. It originates from the region of Shaoxing, in the Zhejiang province of eastern China. It is widely used as both a beverage and a cooking wine in Chinese cuisine.

Shrimp paste (or belachan) is made from fermented ground shrimp, sun-dried and either cut into fist-sized rectangular blocks or sold in bulk. It is an essential ingredient in many curries and sauces and is a common ingredient used in Southeast Asian and Southern Chinese cuisine.

Slippery elm powder. This powder is made from the dried and ground inner bark of the slippery elm tree (*Ulmus rubra*.) It can be used to increase your daily fibre intake and may have a soothing effect on the digestive system. Slippery elm powder is commonly recommended to provide relief from sore throats, constipation, diarrhoea and other symptoms of an irritated digestive tract such as bloating. It can be made into a gruel, stirred into a glass of water or made into a soothing tea.

Spelt is an old variety of wheat originating in Persia. It contains gluten but is easily digested. It is high in protein and has immune-boosting properties.

Sumac. The fruits of the genus *Rhus* are ground into a deep-red or purple powder used as a spice in Middle Eastern cuisine to add a lemony taste to salads or meat. In Arab cuisine, it is used as a garnish on mezé dishes such as hummus and is added to salads. In Iranian cuisine, sumac is added to rice or kebabs. In Turkish cuisine, it is added to salad servings of kebabs and lahmacun. *Rhus coriaria* is used in the spice mixture zaatar.

Tahini is made from ground, lightly toasted sesame seeds and is available hulled or unhulled. The former has had its husks removed and the latter is used to make East Asian sesame paste. Gluten free.

Taklia. A paste made up of ground coriander, garlic, olive oil and salt. Used as a condiment in Middle Eastern cuisine.

Tamari is a good-quality soy sauce from Japan. It is made using fermented soybeans and sea salt. Gluten free.

Tempeh is a fermented soy product from Indonesia. It is high in protein and easy to digest. Gluten free.

Tomato passata is sieved uncooked tomatoes. It usually has the skin, seeds, leaves and stems removed.

Tofu is an unfermented soy product high in protein and great for the spleen and stomach as well as for stabilising blood sugar. Low in fat. Available as firm, soft, silken or smoked. Gluten free.

Turmeric (*Curcuma longa*) is part of the ginger family and is native to tropical South Asia. The root is available fresh. It looks like ginger but not as wide and has a beautiful, deep-yellow colour inside. When not used fresh, the rhizomes are boiled for several hours and then dried in hot ovens, after which they are ground into a deep orange-yellow powder. The powder is commonly used as a spice in curries and other South Asian and Middle Eastern cuisine, for dyeing, and to impart colour to mustard condiments. Its active ingredient is curcumin and it has a distinctly earthy, slightly bitter, slightly hot, peppery flavor and a mustardy smell. It has been used for 4000 years to treat a variety of conditions. Studies show that turmeric may help fight infections and some cancers, reduce inflammation, and treat digestive problems.

Umeboshi. These salted pickled plums (actually an apricot) have the effect of reducing acid in the body when eaten. The plums can be bought whole, and are also available as a vinegar or paste. Gluten free.

Wakame is a sea vegetable, or edible seaweed. It has a subtly sweet flavour and is most often served in soups and salads. New studies have found that a compound in wakame known as fucoxanthin can help burn fatty tissue. In Oriental medicine it has been used for blood purification, intestinal strength, skin, hair, reproductive organs and menstrual regularity. Gluten free.

Wood ear fungus. This can refer to two different, closely related species of edible fungus used primarily in Asian cuisine. These are commonly sold in Asian markets shredded and dried.

Index

Acknowledgements

I would like to thank Melrose Foods and Loving Earth; and Byron Bay retail stores Bay Seafood, Red Ginger, Little Peach and Our Corner Store for their generous support of this book.